T0195000

CHURCHED AND BROKEN

Through the Eyes of a Child

CAROLYN V. WEBB

WESTBOW
PRESS®
A DIVISION OF THOMAS NELSON
& ZONDERVAN

This book is a work of non-fiction. Unless otherwise noted, the author and the publisher make no explicit guarantees as to the accuracy of the information contained in this book and in some cases, names of people and places have been altered to protect their privacy.

WestBow Press books may be ordered through booksellers or by contacting:

WestBow Press
A Division of Thomas Nelson & Zondervan
1663 Liberty Drive
Bloomington, IN 47403
www.westbowpress.com
844-714-3454

Because of the dynamic nature of the Internet, any web addresses or links contained in this book may have changed since publication and may no longer be valid. The views expressed in this work are solely those of the author and do not necessarily reflect the views of the publisher, and the publisher hereby disclaims any responsibility for them.

Any people depicted in stock imagery provided by Getty Images are models, and such images are being used for illustrative purposes only. Certain stock imagery © Getty Images.

Scripture taken from the King James Version of the Bible.

Taken from the HOLY BIBLE: EASY-TO-READ VERSION © 2014 by Bible League International. Used by permission.

Scripture taken from The Message. Copyright © 1993, 1994, 1995, 1996, 2000, 2001, 2002. Used by permission of NavPress Publishing Group.

ISBN: 978-1-6642-8625-2 (sc)
ISBN: 978-1-6642-8624-5 (hc)
ISBN: 978-1-6642-8623-8 (e)

Library of Congress Control Number: 2022922685

Print information available on the last page.

WestBow Press rev. date: 1/18/2023

CONTENTS

DISCLAIMER

The controversial prose within this book is designed to evoke change.

Change us, oh God, so that we may worship You.

This book is dedicated to Christian believers who have worn masks for years to hide the pain of spiritual brokenness. Brokenness is so prevalent in the lives of believers. This book offers a safe place where we can reveal, discuss, and make the necessary adjustments. Let us begin to understand why we use masks. Let us understand that children of God do not need masks. Let us move into the destined purpose God has for our lives.

Churched and broken at the same time? How can one be a saved active member of a church, know all the religious jargon, and be broken? Shall we?

Spiritual brokenness is a result of getting sucker-punched by those who claim to love us, getting kicked in the gut by family or church members, or simply being overwhelmed with the cares of life. Spiritual brokenness causes us to be separated from God. Many of our worst hurts come from the mouths of family and church members. Scars from those we hold in high esteem. Brokenness is the driving force our spirit uses to lead us to the intervention of God. We realize we are desperately dependent upon God, and without him, we can do nothing.

Brokenness consists of many facets. One aspect of brokenness involves an introspective look at ourselves. Brokenness forces us to look at those hidden offenses towards ourselves. Let us uncover how we hurt others and ourselves with our emotions, thoughts, posture, and decisions. God uses brokenness to restore us.

Only God can remove the mask we don to camouflage our pain. Off with the masks.

A broken spirit leaves one with a feeling of grief, shame, pain, no hope for the future, powerlessness, and helplessness. Brokenness leaves one feeling defeated, discouraged, and in desperate need of truth, encouragement, and restoration.
Brokenness renders our hearts pliable, humble, and vulnerable. Brokenness opens us to the Word of God. It is through brokenness God shows us the character flaws we otherwise ignore.

A broken spirit leaves a broken and contrite heart, submerged with guilt and remorse. A broken spirit points us to God as our only option.

PSALM 34:18

The Lord is nigh [near or close] unto them that are of a broken heart and saves such as be of a contrite heart. (KJV)

The Lord is close to those who have suffered disappointment. He saves those who are discouraged. (ERV)

If your heart is broken, you will find God right there; if you are kicked in the gut, he will help you catch your breath. (Message Bible)

Jesus suffered brokenness on the cross, and he knows all too well about brokenness. Jesus holds redemptive power to give us beauty for our ashes. Let us allow our brokenness to drive and direct us into the presence of the only wise God.

Our trials and life crises do not change God's character but force us to seek changes in our lives, changes to our thought processes, and changes that shall make a difference.

Romans 8:30 says God justifies us and makes us righteous in the sight of God as if we never sinned. In addition to the justification comes the promise of glorification that one day, we will stand completely purged of any sin.

PROLOGUE: SPIRITUAL MASK

Travel with Nita as she revisits her childhood to find the cause of her brokenness. Go back as Nita learns the root of her trauma, the beginning of donning a mask to camouflage pain. Discover with Nita the purpose of the undeveloped seed left in her childhood. Come along and learn how we can be churched and broken.

Nita loved the Lord and trusted in his Word, yet she was broken. Churched and broken. She was an articulate, intelligent, and loving person. Beneath the bells and whistles was a broken little girl with an attitude. Her attitude was the biggest part of her personality. Her posture could put one on notice without effort. A little girl who desired to be validated. She decided to use her spiritual imagination to unveil the root cause of her brokenness. What caused her to have an attitude? Was she born with it? Where did the arrogance come from? Where did she learn the art of indifference?
All questions that required answers: the when, why, where, and how come?

Nita thought all Christian believers must be broken in some way and wanted to find where her brokenness began. Her curiosity prompted her to investigate and revisit her childhood. She went as far back as she could remember, only to find that she had mastered the art of camouflage, the gift of masking her true feelings. Nita suffered from anxiety and over-compulsive disorder. Such difficulty in understanding how one could fellowship every Sunday and hide behind the mask of material things was amazing to her. In the house, churched and still broken. What is going on with this brokenness?

Put it on the table.
Is there one who shall escape this life without an encounter with brokenness? No, brokenness is universal. Brokenness does not

discriminate. The world operates on brokenness. Brokenness seeks a specialist. Brokenness shows itself through the mass shootings of innocent children and elderly citizens. Brokenness shows itself in a society that is comfortable with homelessness and mental illness.

Brokenness requires someone who specializes in healing broken people. Perhaps a high priest? Possibly a Shepherd? Maybe a cross-bearing Savior? Jesus has authority over brokenness. Through the cross, Jesus knows all about brokenness.

Surely, he was wounded for our transgressions and bruised for our iniquities.

God is near or close to those of us who have suffered disappointment, those who have broken hearts, and those who have been kicked in the gut and discouraged. God will help us catch our breath. We must go to him for daily restoration. God is the Master over brokenness.

CHAPTER 1

BROKEN IMAGE VERSUS DISCIPLESHIP

In the beginning, was the Word, and the Word opened Nita's eyes to understanding.

Nita loathed the patent leather shoes she had to wear each year on Resurrection Sunday, formerly known as Easter. The shoes were either too tight and pinched her toes or too big and constantly slipped off her foot. The lace net slip beneath the Easter dress itched horribly as if the shoes were not enough to torture.

Nita and her sister Ann fidgeted during the wait to recite their Easter speeches.

Ann asked, "Do you think God wanted us to wear these slippery shoes and itchy dresses?"

"Shush," said the usher. "You know better to talk in God's house."

Nita eyed Ann and whispered, "We came to talk," as they giggled quietly. They did not want to miss out on the Easter baskets full of candy and eggs.

Nita's eldest brother explained to them that eggs and candy had nothing to do with the resurrection of Christ.

"Well, why do we go through this every year?" Nita asked.

"Such the little attitude," her brother said.

Each year, with precision, their eldest brother Lewis, and his wife collected Nita and Ann for Easter shopping. Nita would always go back and forth with her brother about the patent leather shoes.

"Why do I have to wear these shoes? I don't like this dress, either."

"You will wear them, so keep quiet."

Nita would always whisper to Ann, "He is not the boss of me."

The sisters knew well the church's departments, boards, and circles. Attending Sunday school, choir rehearsal, and Bible study were requirements for Nita and Ann. They often remembered the prayers of deacons, as some were repetitive in nature. The church was a second home for Nita and Ann. Dad's detachment to church was shown by his knock on the church door upon picking us up.

The church had many human-made rules and regulations with no biblical foundation. Nita thought maybe the rules were the reason people joined in droves and disappeared in droves. What happened? Nita fellowshipped every Sunday with other believers, going through the motions, but everyone seemed to be broken in some way. The pain was unspoken, yet real. Something was missing.

Could unforgiveness be a component of brokenness? Anxiety? Unaddressed issues? Attitudes? Childhood trauma? There was an overwhelming feeling of brokenness exuding from the believers.

Members appeared to be more interested in the image they portrayed rather than being their authentic selves. The focus was more on how they looked, what they wore, where they lived, *and even how they worshipped.* Members focused on how they wanted others to think about them. No real tangible evidence spoke to their Christianity. While members looked at outward appearances, God continues to look at the heart.

Such human-made ideas were passed down from generation to generation, creating more broken Christians hiding behind a pious façade of righteousness. Material things caught the congregation's attention, suggesting these members were blessed. It appeared blessings were connected to material things. The more material things one had, the more blessed one was thought to be. We were subliminally taught to look down on those who did not fit into the hypocritical circles we formed within the walls of fellowship. The image showed up one way, and the believer's actions overruled the images. The image was a fading snapshot, containing no virtue or substance.

Without a doubt, Jesus was the main attraction on Resurrection Sunday (Easter), Christmas, Communion, funerals, and during the Pastor's sermons on Sunday.
It had to be your experience to know the difficulty and struggle to maintain this façade. More focus was placed on the image of looking pious rather than being an effective disciple.

Nita and Ann attended Sunday school, Bible study, and their mother's circle meetings. They were often the only children among the adults. Nita loved being with the adults; there was so much to learn and know. The older Christian women had knowledge and game, so Nita embraced them.
Besides, Nita felt she was an adult. She thought maybe this had something to do with the brokenness of the members.

She was curious to find out. To Nita's disappointment, the topic was always about food boxes for the less fortunate, scholarships, and prayers for the sick.
Nevertheless, Nita loved being in their presence. It was from this circle Nita came to love older women. The older women were full of wisdom and confidence. Many of the hats worn by the ladies demanded confidence. The hats were very colorful, to say the least.

The ladies of the circle had nerves of steel, a requirement for the hats they donned. Ann inherited the wearing of big hats and suits from their mom.
All the ladies of the circle had many suits, hats with matching handbags, and shoes. The image of the time. Nita preferred the comfort of being free.

Nita thought, *if we are to be in church all day, we should be comfortable first, and well put together, second. We adopt habits extended by our exposure.*

The downside to the image was the crippling effect it had on some. Crippling, as it caused them not to utilize their God-given talents. It caused others to sink into their shells, feeling inadequate to compete with the hype. Some hit despair in the attempt to keep an image going. Others chose not to participate due to the gossiping and hypocritical spirits hiding behind the mask of some believers.

The idea of keeping it real was another mask for gossip. Christians must be careful of the subtle tricks of the enemy. Our posture of authenticity should not center around telling the business of others or creating a negative narrative about others. The truth of the matter is, gossiping and being authentic are opposite ends of the spectrum. Authenticity involves genuineness and should not be confused with gossiping.

Becoming your authentic self is liberating and frees you to love yourself and be comfortable with who you are and where you are in life. Authenticity allows you to embrace your good and work on your not-so-good. Embracing oneself first makes it easier to embrace others. Embracing your authentic self removes doubt, insecurity, and the judgment of others. We must ask ourselves a few questions before we put our mouths on another. Will my comment help anyone? Is my light shining? Does my comment encourage or uplift? If the answer is no, we should keep our comments to ourselves. Giving another a piece of your mind is not authentic but is rooted in carnality. We need the full capacity of our minds with the helmet of salvation to protect and keep God in our thoughts.

When we stand before God's judgment, we will be judged on our stewardship, how we treated each other, and if we shared the Good News of Jesus.

It is through the guidance of the Holy Spirit that we learn to embrace everyone, even when they don't move or speak in the same manner as we do. Jesus embraced everyone, regardless of their spiritual level. Nita's bottom line was, none of us possess heaven or hell for anyone, not even ourselves.

Imagery is a trick of the devil. The image takes our focus from what is important, our very own brokenness. We can mask ourselves behind the latest fashions and the latest hairstyle and come across as the next top model, but without love, without compassion, we become as sounding brass or a tingling cymbal.

Many of us have fallen or been trapped into believing image is more important than substance, due to the brokenness of our spirits.

Imagery is a temporary glimpse that fades away. Imagery is one of the masks used to camouflage brokenness.

CHAPTER 2

CHILDHOOD TRAUMA AND ATTITUDE

Nita unraveled her brokenness.

At this point, Nita was convinced most people did not realize they were broken. Most have adjusted to a mediocre level of existence, living through the survival mode the world offers. We have become comfortable in survival mode, and thus we are unable to recognize God's peace. All effort goes into keeping the image.

Sunday school and Bible study were Nita's favorites. The Word of God intrigued her at an early age. Nita's first Bible was one with pictures. She believed this Bible helped her become a literal, visual learner. She could receive a Word, and a panoramic view of that Word would follow. She had question after question. Did God instruct us to follow all these rules with no joy? Did he desire us to obey the letter of the law with no peace? Did he just want these images of Christian believers and no real substance? Did he watch over us with a big belt, waiting for us to make a mistake so he could punish us? It was all so confusing when the believer's behavior did not match their words.

Oftentimes, Nita's anxious thoughts would suggest she miss a couple of Sundays. Maybe she could even stop praying. Fellowship was so ingrained in Nita's spirit that stopping was not an option. Bible study, praying, and fellowshipping with other believers were the very things that brought peace and hope to her spirit. Yet the brokenness taunted Nita more than she cared to admit. She needed a breakthrough of understanding. She needed to understand why believers thought image to be more important than being their authentic selves.

Pastor Gregory D. Hunter tells us salvation is free, but discipleship is costly. Believers must break away from the imagery, unlearn those human-made rules and rituals, and move into becoming more of a disciple of substance, authentic in those things that speak power and encouragement to others. Christian believers are the only Bible some will ever read, so we must make sure our behavior and actions align together. Practicing the same message we preach is crucial.

We must return to our origin, reboot, and start all over again.
Travel back in time with Nita, back into the mind of that little boy or girl, back to the root of your trauma, pain, and disappointments. To address childhood pain, you must admit there was trauma. God has specially blessed you if you have no childhood trauma. Continue to be blessed. Those of us who have experienced childhood trauma will need to call upon our faith in God. You need to utilize your relationship with God. You need to tap into your spiritual imagination.

Finally, you will need a mirror of some sort to view yourself and release yourself from past hurts. The first step is to look closely at yourself in the mirror, I mean down into the pupil of your eyes, until you see yourself, your reflection. You may appear to look a little tired and weary, only because so much time has elapsed since you've taken a good look at yourself. It's okay because you are about to be free indeed.

Most of us barely glance at our true selves in the mirror. Once we connect with the image we wish to portray, our soul search ends. Push past the image until you see your younger self waiting with open arms for your attention. Look until you see yourself. Your younger self may be a little on the needy side because you masked up a long time ago and forced-fed scraps to your seed. We taught our seed to operate in survival mode, leaving that undeveloped seed desperately in want.

The first thing you must do is forgive yourself. Forgive yourself for *all* the times you gave your joy away. We have heard it said we won't allow others to steal our joy. Joy is intangible, internal, a posture we relinquish. We need our joy to experience the fullness of God's presence. Forgive yourself for the many times you hid your purpose and minimized your self-worth. Forgive yourself for the time wasted trying to fit in with the world's system. Forgive yourself for trusting people more than trusting God. Forgive yourself for the times you tried to live up to the expectations of others. Forgive yourself for receiving all the negative words spoken to and against you. Forgive the statement that sticks, and stones may break our bones, but words will never hurt. Those words did hurt; they crippled and stamped insecurity on our self-esteem. Forgive yourself for believing lies as the norm. Forgive your parents for the regimented upbringing; our parents had no blueprint and thus could only give their children the benefit of what they knew.

Now that we know better, we shall do better. Forgive yourself for minimizing yourself to be accepted. We have worn masks for so long that we have forgotten who we are. We have embraced our trauma until we no longer recognize the strength God has given us. We have forgotten we are representatives, ambassadors, and disciples of Christ on the earth.

You will never know just how strong you are until you forgive people who are not sorry for their actions, accepting an apology from their lips only (let that sit in your spirit). Forgive yourself for thinking your happiness was controlled by someone else. You must control the thermostat of your emotions, and you can only do that by applying the Word of God.

We constantly ask for peace but are unable to embrace it because our focus always returns to the residue of the trauma. Trauma is familiar. Forgive the mask you created to protect yourself. Forgive yourself for responding to the null and void comments offered by others. Listen, when you get to a place where only what God says about you is important, then only what God says will matter. I believe that to be a place of perfect peace.

Forgive yourself for holding grudges. Only the Word of God is so essential that you must hold on to it. Unforgiveness and grudges negate the Word of God. Forgive yourself for seeking revenge; revenge simply wants to get even. Revenge wants another to feel what you felt; it is not justice. 'Vengeance is Mine saith the Lord' (Romans 12:19 KJV). Utilize all the forgiveness you need, to free yourself of anything that held your emotions hostage. Plead the blood of Jesus over yourself. It is difficult to love someone who is broken, especially if that someone is you, me, or us. We must first learn to forgive ourselves.

Allow your tears to flow, release them. Tears are our words unspoken in the spirit. Tears are the spiritual language of God; only God knows the sentiment behind our tears. Tears are our private conversations with God. Let the tears flow as you release those emotions which bound you for years. Allow your tears to cleanse and purge the toxic waste from your spirit. "Purge us with hyssop and we shall be clean; wash us and we shall be whiter than snow." Some will never admit or acknowledge their part in the conflict. They may not be ready. Forgive yourself for disliking those who challenged you, those who emotionally bullied or taunted you.

If you can, admit you are broken. If you can, acknowledge your role in the conflict. This is the place where God can take your brokenness and realign you back to his original plan for your life. You have grown in the spirit when you can accept an apology you never received. Forgiving yourself first allows you to forgive others. Forgiving yourself allows you to see yourself in a different light.

You realize those things you thought were important are of no value at all. Evict that incident or person out of your spirit; they have squatted too long in your thoughts and emotions.

Secondly, forgive those adults, family, and church members who spoke negatively into your spirit. Once again, people can only tell you what they know and only direct you on a path they have experienced. Forgive whoever violated you and robbed you of your innocence. Most sexual, emotional, and physical trauma are manifestations of the offender's experience. Your part was collateral damage to the experience, no fault of your own.

Collateral damage traumatizes and forces you to relive the incident. Reliving the incident teaches you to torture yourself with your thoughts and blame yourself for things which you had no control over.
Collateral damage crippled your thought process, causing you to relive the trauma over and over in your mind. We must keep our helmets of salvation on to divert the darts of the enemy. Forgiving others removes the powering grip from our thoughts and emotions.

We must release and expel the toxicity before it seeps into our bloodstream. Forgive those who planted negative narratives about you and your self-worth. They may be repeating the very words spoken to them. We must ask for discernment to spiritually break down words that do not speak into our destiny. Discernment offers insight into those words that made us question our purpose. Get thee behind us, Satan. Forgive those who identified you with labels. Those labels were the extent of their understanding and vocabulary. Demonizing the offender only highlights the trauma of your narrative; it will not free your spirit. Once you remove your attention from a person, place, or thing, it no longer has any power. Your *attention* was the driving force all the time.

The purpose of those labels was to classify or identify you negatively. Nita's mom would tell her children when they point the finger at someone, they are three times as bad or guilty. The proof is in the gesture of our hands. Once again trying to make others fit into the boxes of our little minds. Two people can look at the same picture and come away with different perspectives. It does not make either of them right or wrong; it simply speaks to their individuality.
Forgive those who prematurely exposed you to issues your maturity did not understand. Forgive them for not knowing how to explain or direct you through your trauma. If this is where you are today, pray and ask God to release any residue of the trauma. There are so many things Christian believers need to unlearn in the process of getting to their truth.

We must be open to the process. The process is uncomfortable but needed. Through the Holy Spirit, we can take an introspective look inside and wipe the slate clean. Forgive those who lied to you and about you. Lies sell faster than the truth. Lies don't require proof, simply gossiping mouths to keep repeating the narrative.

The truth requires a change of thought and action. The truth is too much work for some, so lies work faster and better. Forgive those who abandoned you; they probably were abandoned and were never taught the principle of faithfulness, dependability, responsibility, and consistency. They were never taught how to stay.

Forgive those who taught you that love comes with conditions. Forgive those who did not fully know your love language. Forgive yourself for not knowing how to articulate your love language. Forgive them for yourself. You may not forget, but you must forgive so you can stay in the process of moving. Let those tears cleanse you into a place of peace, God's perfect peace. Most behavior is learned; you must know better to do better. We are all victims of our socialization, good, bad, or otherwise.

Take control of your thoughts, and your emotions, and yield them to the Holy Spirit and the Word. Focus on those things God has said and what he promised in his Word concerning you. Forgiving others frees you.

God continues to tug on our heartstrings through a pandemic. Most assuredly, our trials and disappointments are how he gets our attention. We can remove our masks and allow him to restore us to him. We can breathe in his presence. We can rest in him as he continues to lead us beside the still waters, restoring our souls daily under his watchful care (Psalm 23).

Finally, thank God for protecting you from the tricks and schemes sent to destroy you. Thank God for blessing you to overcome. Thank God the trial was not unto death. Thank God you are still on assignment. Thank God you are free of your past hurt and trauma. (Repeat steps one and two until it happens.)

Thank God you did not commit suicide. Thank God you are fearfully and wonderfully made. Thank God he chose to keep you among the living. Give thanks every day because your story could be different. Not everyone made it to this stage of life, so start loving yourself. God placed spiritual value within you. You can begin today.

You are so blessed, so anointed, so kind, so beautiful, and so loved. Repeat the following to yourself every day:

"I love you.

"I love you."

You love you. Include it in your devotional time.

Continue to love yourself and continue to encourage yourself; charity always begins at home. Look into your eyes and tell yourself that you love yourself. Say it until you believe it. Say it until your mind changes regarding how you feel about yourself. Say it until your standards change on the boundaries you need to set. Say it until you begin to change your expectations.

When we learn to love ourselves first, new boundaries come with the package. We can freely love others because we love ourselves. We are blessed to realize it takes nothing away from us to love; it only enhances our witness. We don't lose cool points or credibility; we can now walk in "so" love.

Confirm the love you have for yourself, every day. It is impossible to love others without loving yourself first. The more we see and feel God's love, the more we learn to love ourselves and thus fulfill the great commandments: loving the Lord and then loving our neighbors as we love ourselves. We have been hiding behind masks for too long.

Off with the masks.

Continue to press towards the mark of the higher calling of your life. The enemy knew your potential; the enemy knew God placed spiritual value deep down within you. The enemy kept you distracted and focused on your shoulda, coulda, and woulda. The enemy kept you in your pity parties. The enemy used everything he had to destroy you, "But God."

If you are reading this book, Hallelujah, the enemy lost!
Now tap into it. Tap into that fearfully and wonderfully made disciple God destined you to be. The little boy or girl is free because your life was in God's hands. God has a purpose assigned just for you. The enemy only caused distractions and delays. The enemy could not stop or negate the will of God for your life.

Finally, pick up your seed of destiny. Pick it up and brush off the grime until you see the diamond that you truly are. Nourish that seed, water it with prayer, and build your foundation solid with the Word of God. Nourish your seed so you may fulfill your godly destiny and purpose.

Your purpose is hiding deep in that undeveloped seed left in your childhood. Everything we do in life depends on that seed. The world preyed on your innocence, and your immaturity. The enemy distracted you from the spiritual wisdom inside you. Allow your spiritual growth to put the devil on notice that he is a liar.

Nita's dad was most loving and stern, at the same time. He said what he meant and meant what he said, period. Nita imagined he learned that from the military. Her father was very regimented and precise in his thinking. Nita's household was run in a regimented way. No nonsense was his way. Nita's regimented thought process and her attitude all came from her dad: little sister soldier. Nita later experienced great mental anguish due to her regimented upbringing. We are extensions of our parents, extensions of our exposures. Nita says what she means and means what she says (oftentimes without a filter).

Nita's love for the Word and compassion for the underdog came from her mom. The dynamics of her household promoted teamwork among the siblings. Nita and Ann, being younger, had to follow the directives of their older siblings. Nita always questioned her older sibling's authority, obeying, but not without a fight. If something did not make sense, she questioned it. Nita's questioning came across as a challenge to her older siblings. She received much pleasure in making her older siblings uncomfortable. It was in exchange for the constant orders of being told to do this and do that. The older siblings did not like the barrage of questions daily asked of Nita. How will one know if they do not ask? Nita always asked questions of her brothers. Nita's older brother, Lewis would encourage Nita to "go read a book" when fully annoyed with her. Hah, was this punishment? Nita thought. Nita enjoyed reading and gladly complied.

The shaping of Nita's anxious attitude began with her regimented upbringing. A regimented mindset seeks perfection which no human can achieve!

Nita's brother Lewis introduced the younger siblings to a white-flocked Christmas Tree. It was the first time they had ever seen this type of tree. They were in awe of the beauty of the tree, the Nativity scene, and the beautiful decorations. The white-flocked tree made Christmas special for Nita and Ann. The house would simply light up and the atmosphere would change. Siblings were able to relax; at ease if you will.

Relax to enjoy the music and laughter. Nita loved to laugh. They would cheer and clap in excitement, then sit for hours staring at the tree. The beauty of Christmas, lights, and decorations is a real wonder to behold. Nita and Ann would count the number of presents and hope the wrapped boxes housed what they wished for.

They would make every excuse not to go to bed on Christmas Eve. If they begged long enough, they were able to open one present. A tradition that passed itself down to the next generation.

Nita and Ann did not realize their father was dying (congestive heart failure) and their mother was sick (cancer). Nita did not understand at that time the older siblings were grieving in addition to keeping them in line.

The two older brothers were grieving and preparing to stand in their father's shoes. Each one is respectful in the Army and the Marines. Regimented thinking was something Nita could not shake, it surrounded her. Decent and in order. There must be order, their father would say. Show no sign of weakness. Nita would ask her sister, Ann, "Are we, Stepford children?"

Nevertheless, it was the older siblings' job to keep Nita and her sister Ann busy and protected. The siblings followed orders very well. Nita filed in her memory there were no stipulations or boundaries set upon their baby brother. He was allowed to move independently with fewer rules. "Umm!"

Family business remained in the house, so many things were not discussed in front of them as a protective mechanism. Nita understood the need to protect the younger ones from premature exposure, but she still desired to know.

Nita believed keeping secrets teaches children to lie and hide the truth. Protective mechanisms unknowingly train children how to mask up. We have given the color white to the lies we feel are harmless. No matter the color, a lie is a distortion of the truth. Life issues should be shared and explained to children by their level of understanding, Nita thought.

The older siblings had charge of Nita and Ann. The older siblings controlled their curfew, their friends, what they wore, and bedtime. Nita remembered during family meetings, that her dad would always say, "One for all and all for one." Nita often thought, *we are not in the military, sir*; however, they adapted to the regiment.

The regimented process was a bit much at times, but his children knew how to fall in line. The military term used for relaxing is at ease; Nita felt her dad and brothers could use some at ease time. Nita better understood the mindsets of her other siblings; the regimented upbringing was too much for some of her siblings. In hindsight, Nita desired to thank her father for training his children to be responsible. There was always an abundance of rules with love, support, and encouragement. We, the children, understood boundaries. Did I mention plenty of food? Always plenty of food. There was so much cooking going on that Nita thought the kitchen was a restaurant.

Nita's mother prepared a dessert with each meal. Nita so enjoyed the cakes, pies, and ice cream, pre-diabetes in the making. Nita's mom washed and cleaned all the time. Clean clothes were high on her list. Nita is a compulsive cleaner to this day, almost a compulsive disorder. The disorder makes Nita anxious and uncomfortable.

A place for everything, and everything in its place. Nita's mindset and ideas function in this regiment. Nita's mother did not work outside of the home; her job was raising her children. The church was the primary outside for her mother. Nita thought when she grows up, she will have a career outside of the home and be her boss. She would not depend on any man to take care of her, not even her husband. Nita loved how her parents supported each other; however, she wished to see her mom disagree or challenge her dad, just once.

The shaping of Nita's attitude prompted her to question authority and independence. Each of her siblings knew their assignment, and no one stepped outside of their role. At least not while Dad was alive. Time did not offer the opportunity for sibling rivalry because everyone was following orders. Nita thought she and her sister Ann were in the military as well, left, right, left. The regiment laid down rules, and the consequences of breaking those rules were scary. Who wanted a confrontation with Dad? Nita's brothers outnumbered dad, yet no one challenged him. This convinced Nita that dads are not only the head of the house but are needed in the house for balance. Well at least in Nita's case.

Never was there a spanking or whipping from Dad or Mom, which convinced Nita there were no signs of child abuse. Nita could not find any bruises, burns, or scratches when she examined her body. Nita's older siblings would tell the story of Nita having a metal plate in her head. They went on to tell Nita she was mentally challenged, and all the siblings were trained to treat her as if she was normal. Of course, Nita never believed this story and learned to laugh at herself along with her other siblings. She believed she was off-limits because of her attitude and quick mouth. She was thought to have more of the father's spirit than any of her siblings.

Nita's dad dipped snuff, and on occasion, he would signal to one of his children to bring his chewing tobacco can. Nita would say to the designated sibling, "Let Dad get his can; he can walk." Everyone would burst into laughter, including Dad. All would say in unison, that metal plate in her head. Of course, Nita laughed with them.

There was an occasion with a childhood infraction, and Nita's brother Lewis thought he would physically chastise his younger sisters. Nita was enraged by this decision and spoke for herself and her sister. Lewis approached them with a belt. Nita asked her brother, "What in the world is wrong with you? You know boys are not supposed to hit girls, at least that is what you tell us. How do you expect me to believe your words when you don't practice them?"
Nita told Lewis he was being a bully and used his own words to shame him. She said she would call 911 on him. Nita heard of an organization called Child Protective Services, and she did not have a problem contacting them.
Nita touched Lewis' vulnerability, and the pending whipping was avoided. Praise the Lord. Nita thought her brother probably needed a nap or something. Ann was crying in fear of the pending whipping. Nita's brothers possessed advanced boxing skills under their belts. This training was picked up from the military. A fight should be matched fairly. The threat of a whipping did not offer a level fighting field. Nita hugged Ann and said, "He is just tired; don't worry, there will be no whippings today."

The threat of a whipping was the tool Lewis chose to scare his younger siblings into obedience. The whipping threat is where Nita learned one of her boundaries. "I may not comply with your wishes;

however, I will listen to you. You can talk to me, you can talk about me, but never put your hands on me."

Nita expressed to her brother she would make the effort to work with him, but she was offended he chose to abuse the authority given to him as an older brother. Nita was thankful her older siblings took good care of the younger children and understood she and Ann could present a challenge.

My public service announcement to the younger generation is to be thankful you have parents who care for and about you. Parents deserve credit for doing the best they can. Enjoy them while you have them. Take the time to ask your parents about their childhood, dreams, aspirations, and goals. Most parents deferred their dreams and aspirations so their children may have better opportunities.
Stop assuming you know everything about them; trust me, you don't. If you don't ask them, you will never know. A day is coming when they will no longer be with you. Believe me, it will leave a crater of a hole in your heart. Stop wasting time trying to correct, criticize, and find fault with your parents. Love and respect are owed to your parents, no matter what. Nita is old school for real. We are thriving today on the prayers of our parents and grandparents.

Nita loved and respected her parents. She was thankful for them. Through her parents, she learned to respect adults. Nita thought it to be a sign of brokenness when adults stepped out of their place of authority and respect.

Nita's childhood regimen believed even adults should know and maintain their place. Left, right, left. The regimented unity and precision were directives of Dad. Softness, kindness, and compassion from her mom. We were taught to band together, and together we did. Encouraged to support and protect the other at the end of the day, good, bad, or otherwise.

Nita needed balance. The idea of balance forced her to adjust, and her anxiety continued to grow. Her upbringing forced her to become astutely observant, to listen as much as she talked, observe the omitted, and watch the actions of others.
Listen, not only to hear but listen for understanding. We have two ears. Look for the things not shown and listen for things not said. Nita felt she was a detective. Turns out this was one of her gifts. The ability to break down context became most important, all driven by her anxiety. God can even use anxiety!

Philippians 4:6, be anxious for nothing but in everything by prayer and supplication with thanksgiving make your request known unto God. (KJV)
became Nita's daily; mantra. Throughout the day, she learned to tell herself to be anxious for nothing, be anxious for nothing. Nita's brother Lewis always referred to Nita as an Alpha female.

Nita felt her brother was attempting to insult her with one of his military phrases, which prompted her to look the word up.
An alpha female tends to

- believe her ability to achieve is limitless,
- have a contagious confidence, which leads others to respect her as an equal,
- showcase leadership characteristics,
- be recognized by others as being impactful, and
- have extremely high ambitions.

Upon researching the phrase, Nita realized her brother had more wisdom and discernment than she credited to him.

The dynamics of life look different outside the safety of your home. Nita had to learn how to maneuver outside of the regimented safety of her brothers and sister. You must learn to secure your perspective despite the dynamics of the world.

Being in the world and not of the world requires precision and balance. Only Christ offers precision and balance.

Although Nita accepted Christ at an early age, she was still growing into Christian maturity. Personal experiences accelerated her relationship with Christ. Trials of life forced her into the safe arms of Jesus.

Sickness and death were the events where Nita came to personally know Jesus. She had visions of her mother's death before it happened. Nightmare after nightmare of the funeral service. She thought to herself, *what will I do if my mother passes? How would life go on? What would life look like?*

Nita remembered the blood-curdling screams her mom made throughout the night. The pain was real. A mother is your first best friend. Anxiety intensified. Nita was not skilled in understanding her visions or how to proceed, so she went into mute caretaker mode. Jesus used the death of her mother to woo and comfort Nita through her mental fog. Jesus showed himself as compassionate, kind, loving, and patient, a more intense version of her mother. Jesus knew she needed that.

Nita found Jesus to be a man of his word. He could maneuver and accomplish things no one else could. He appeared to specialize in making ways out of no way. Nita began to keep a journal of her prayer requests and mark the exact day God answered her prayers.

The Holy Spirit gave a few words to this song as an acknowledgment of the wonderful signs and wonders of God.

If it had not been for the Lord, who was on Nita's side, where would she be? He kept my enemies away and let the sunshine through a cloudy day. The favorite part of the song says he rocked Nita in the cradle of his love because he knew, he knew she had been battered and scarred. The storms continued to come, and Jesus was there with each storm, wooing and tugging on the strings of Nita's heart. Opening closed doors, reading her thoughts, answering her prayers before she could get them out of her mouth. Nita was in awe of God's Word, confident in his Word.

Nita found comfort in her secret closet, her place of trysting. If it had not been for the Lord on my side, where would I be?

God used sickness and death to reveal Nita's place of brokenness, a place where her heart was pliable and receptive, a place where he could use her for his kingdom. God does his best work through the brokenness of his people.

Reconciling death is still a very painful process. It never goes away, but with time, it gets easier.

Up against the wall, God is there being the rewarder of those who diligently seek him. God is strategic and detailed in his plan for those who desire to know him.

Could brokenness be a part of God's plan? Is brokenness the posture where God does his best work?

The sacrifice that God wants is a humble spirit. God does not turn away anyone who comes with a humble heart willing to obey him.

CHAPTER 3

SCHOOL TRAUMA
AND ATTITUDE

Did some adult speak negatively into Nita's spirit? Did she digest the negative words? Words are powerful. Didn't Nita have the ability to offer a rebuttal? Was it an adult in authority who tried to minimize her self-worth? The seed of her attitude began to question validation and self-worth.

Nita was accepted into what was then known as the gifted program. The gifted program included a mixture of students from different cultures and ethnicities. These students were viewed as high achievers, and exceptional in academics. Nita's first lesson in the new program was entitlement. During recess, one of the students began to give out assignments and decided who would turn the jump rope and who would jump first (she was Caucasian). Of course, she jumped first, she jumped second, and she jumped third. She jumped until the bell rang, signaling students to line up and return to class. What were we thinking in continuing to turn the rope? The experience was new for the children of color; we could only take mental notes and observe. This classmate added insult to injury and offered Nita two Oreo cookies if she could jump first the following day.
Why did she only ask me? Nita thought. *Was I turning the rope that well?*

Nita politely told her classmate she could not be bought with cookies. Nita suggested the student bring her jump rope, and she could turn and jump all at the same time, all by herself.
Nita scoffed and said as they were taking their seats, "I like chocolate chip cookies, anyway." She filed the incident in the Rolodex of her memory. Entitlement.

Nita witnessed more brokenness from students of her own culture, the students she attended school with, students from her neighborhood, the haves, and the have-nots. This drama was active long before the sitcom. The haves would gossip and look down on the have-nots. The have-nots were criticized daily about their choice of clothes, their lack of style, and their free lunches. These were daily topics. They haves judged the coolness and popularity of everyone. The have-nots did not wear the latest styles or name brands. Designer clothes were not something Nita understood at this point in her life. She did not fully understand how and why clothes were such a big deal. What role did clothes play in one's identity? Image again.

The toxicity of images, even in children, is a learned behavior. Who focuses on children's clothes? If the body and clothes are clean, isn't that all that matters? The have-nots were singled out when they lined up to get free lunch. It was the same menu; some paid, while others ate free. Nita thought it was a divisive practice. She would have gladly taken a free lunch and bought candy with her quarter. She felt she was getting the short end of the stick in this situation. She felt this to be another tool of the system to separate and cause division within an already broken culture. A simple decision of having one student eat free and one student pay immediately questions self-worth. This practice suggested to the haves they were different, if not better.

While Nita knew the haves, she connected with the have-nots. The haves would ask her why she sat at the table with the have-nots; Nita would respond with some flippant answer, and the haves would go away. Nita knew the female haves were nice to her because they were interested in her brothers. The haves was like pests with their constant buzzing about the have-nots; Nita's goals far surpassed clothes and lunches; she had big dreams and plans that would make a difference in people's lives.

Nita was someone who followed her own rules. Her silence was often perceived as being shy or timid when she simply did not wish to be bothered. She was not intimidated by peer pressure. The dynamics are a little different when you hail from a large family.

Nita declared, "I'm here to learn. School is not a fashion show," she would tell the haves, who validated themselves and associated self-worth with material things. "My self-worth is not in my clothes."

"But you dress better than them," the haves would say.

"And that makes me better?" she asked. "Plus, I don't have a job. I wear the clothes my parents provide for me; I do not have a say in what they buy. I imagine it's the same for us all. I'm just happy we no longer must wear uniforms."

Nita enjoyed the food and would have gladly taken a free lunch.

"Ignore them," she would tell the have-nots. "But if they get in your personal space, you know what to do." Another life lesson from Nita's dad.

No limos were parked in front of the school waiting to take any of us back to the projects. We all walked the same path home to the same housing complex. They are shallow and superficial. If they lived outside of this housing complex, I just might subscribe to their beliefs. I see us all in the same situation, free lunch or not.

There were no conversations about a person's clothes or gender in Nita's home. It never crossed Nita's mind that she and Ann were blessed. Everything was taken for granted, as there was never a worry or question about food, clothing, or shelter. Free lunches were never a topic of conversation. Nita's mother did not share her thoughts on those types of issues; they were not important to her mother, and so they were not important to Nita. Nita's mom embraced everyone.

Nita was enamored by God's grace and mercy towards her, his compassion, and his tender loving-kindness towards her. Nita was blessed to have friends who also understood the passion of Christ. God sends angels in disguise to assist us as we maneuver through the process of life. Nita's friends are still in place to this day. Thank God.

Nita's first experience defining her self-worth came from a grade-school English teacher. Nita received an A in her English class. Words were essential to the becoming of Nita. The teacher's attitude toward the students was one of indifference. It spoke loudly. The teacher's lack of encouragement and low expectations of the students followed her into the classroom each day. Despite Nita's good grades, the teacher offered no motivation, no encouragement, and no validation of her existence. She continued to excel anyway. The ability to operate under indifference and still excel heightened Nita's arrogance. Attitude and arrogance proved themselves to be a deadly combination, spawning anxiety. Could this be the reason she was an overachiever? She discovered the public school system was not designed to advance children of color.

Nita did not understand at that time, indifference was shaping her behavior. She was becoming the very thing she disliked. The said teacher falsely accused Nita of being disruptive in class. The teacher informed Nita's mom that Nita needed to apologize to her, receive corporal punishment, and attend summer school to receive a grade she had already earned. Nita also could not participate in the eighth-grade commencement service.

Nita's mom tried to encourage her to accept the conditions, but Nita decided she would wait for her dad's decision in the situation. An apology was out of the question; no apology for something she did not do. No, to the wooden paddle from the male principal. Nita refused to be the main entertainment of some warped fantasy. After all, this teacher never bothered to validate Nita or any of the students. This posture made it easy for her to paint all the students of color with the same brush. Nita did not quite understand all the facets of racial inequality, but she was adamant there was no paddling for her.

Nita's dad made the final decision, and summer school it was. The fact that Nita remembers this incident in detail denotes the trauma. Why would a teacher lie about a student? Why did the teacher choose Nita? There were some disruptive and disrespectful students in the classroom; however, Nita was not one of them. To this day, Nita does not have an answer but wishes God to bless the teacher just the same.

Nita came to know Jesus as her friend. The sacrifice of Jesus dying for the sins of the world on the cross. It is at this point we must discuss Christ's compassion.

When we think about God's love and empathy toward us, it is mind-blowing. The suffering he endured the night before the Crucifixion until his death upon the cross. Christ was the ultimate sacrifice for the world. God's grace offers several benefits: salvation, the forgiveness of sins, a relationship with God, access to God's throne, the ability to endure trials, and the power to sustain our Christian walk.

It is because Jesus was wounded and bruised for us that he fully possesses the power and ability to address our brokenness. God does his best work in us when we are vulnerable and weak. We must put our faith in God's hands. We must trust God, even when we can't see our way. Even when we don't fully understand.

Indifference and lack of acknowledgment defined the sadness Nita also witnessed on the faces of Christian believers. Members said they love the Lord and intentionally walk past each other, not speaking, but more than eager to gossip about each other, whispering under their breath about people as if they are ventriloquists. People see what we are doing; people see us for who we are. *Been there and done that,* thought Nita. Speaking negatively about someone has no reflection on the person but addresses what is in your heart. Remember, we can't judge people from the page we walked in on, or the narrative given by others.

Gossiping is a clear sign of brokenness. Nita saw gossiping as a protective mechanism used to avoid addressing oneself.

Indifference must be a cousin to validation. If I ignore you, you do not exist. The posture of indifference is difficult to shake when adopted at an early age, Nita thought. There was always this stoic look on the faces of her brothers, almost as if they wanted to relax but had to remain in formation. At ease.

Oops. Nita convicted herself and realized she was quite an expert at indifference towards others. She knew all too well how to dismiss people with a straight face.

Due to the regimented atmosphere at home and the indifference of a teacher, Nita recognized the where and the why of her indifference, her stubborn attitude, and her arrogance. A child's mind is like a tape recorder, putting to memory both good and mostly bad experiences. It took an ardent effort to keep this brokenness in place.

The very hurtful things Nita experienced, she was now transmitting to others. Not to excuse or blame the behavior but to acknowledge, discover, and have the desire to unlearn the toxic behavior.

It is hurtful to give your best and not have your efforts acknowledged or appreciated. The pain of learning the support you gave to others was not reciprocated. It is traumatizing when that indifference and lack of support come from family or Christian believers. It is most devastating when it comes from those who are supposed to love you, those you hold in high regard. The pain of a crushed spirit is unbearable. Walking through life angry, holding grudges, and attacking your inner organs. It is not a happy place. We are created for peace. Our bodies and minds release harmful toxins that can destroy us. Emotions need an outlet; when there is no constructive channel of release, the emotions turn and attack the body. It is more harmful to our Christian witness to walk around in stealthy emotions as if everything is okay. We must release those things that bind us.

WHERE IS MY MASK?

Nita was an adolescent; why would a teacher desire to hurt students? Encouraging students is the job of a teacher. Trying to defend yourself against an adult is a challenging scenario, but Nita's dad believed her. Seeking validation from another broken person is futile. Nita's punishment to those who minimized her was to overachieve and ignore them with the gift of her distance. You can know all the scriptures and addresses, but the heart reveals who you are. The heart shows itself, even under a mask. Our actions showcase our hearts. So as a man thinketh in his heart so is he (Proverbs 23:7).

Nita would gladly tell others she had no expectations of them, as they did not register in her scheme of things. It came as a surprise to Nita when people showed decent and kind behavior toward others. She expected the confirmation of ugly words to match the ugly behaviors.

She viewed most as hypocrites and had no confidence in their actions. Not many people practiced what they preached. Most were too busy trying to keep the false image of whom they believed themselves to be.

Lewis asked Nita to consider her words before making broad statements. "You cannot paint everyone with the same brush as the teacher," he said. "Your comment is mean-spirited. Telling someone you have no expectations of them is offensive."

"Brother, my motive is to provoke thought in a way not readily revealed," Nita said.

"I fully understand what you are doing," her brother replied, "which is the reason I don't want you to use that phrase. Words are powerful. Words can build or tear down. You possess the ability to speak powerfully over people, so use your words for good towards others." *Umm*, thought Nita, *he may have something, but he's not my boss.*

This protective mechanism was to protect herself from hurt. Nita felt she would be acknowledged, positively or negatively. Either way, you can't deny I am here. Nita later learned that a person can only give you what they have. People can only take you where they have been and share only what they have experienced. Our parents and grandparents used to say, you can't get blood out of a turnip. Whatever is inside of the heart comes out. Nita was seeking validation in the wrong place and from the wrong people. The teacher did not possess the ability to validate Nita due to his own cultural biases. In the mind of the teacher, none of the students were expected to succeed, and she treated the students accordingly.

Indifference makes one feel invisible and not valued. Indifference says you do not belong. Indifference shows itself in various forms. Indifference sadly shows up in Christian Believers. Brokenness in members of a family, the choir, the deacon board, and even ministers. Broken and churched. Churched and broken.

Christian Believers have an innate desire for acceptance and value from other believers, those regarded in high esteem, a strength in numbers type of thing, a witness from a witness type of fellowship. Believers desire to be among believers who understand and apply the true meaning of fellowship.

When Christian believers are not allowed to fellowship peacefully, it causes division and brokenness. It causes them to question their Christianity and the Christianity of others. Members sit Sunday after Sunday for encouragement, not only by the Word of God but to see an application of the Word, a manifestation of the fruits of the spirit; shouting around the church only to gossip about another member cancels out the witness. Image.

Actions do speak louder than words, in most cases. Are we listening to the same Words the pastor is sharing? Does the Word apply to all? Nita learned that no one on this earth has a monopoly on the mind or spirit of Christ.

If God has no respect for a person, why is Sister So-and-So not included? Should Christians behave differently than God himself? God hates sin and still loves the sinner. Some may say, "I'm not God." So, if you are not God, and I am not God, why are we so critical of each other? Why are we setting worldly standards for others to follow? It all speaks to our state of brokenness. Certainly, we are not God, but our relationship with him should move us to compassion and love for each other. Our relationship with Christ helps us to manifest the fruits of the spirit. Teach us, Holy Spirit.

The cross caused Nita to challenge the motives of her inner thoughts. She had to ask herself, was her faith in humans or God? She learned to pray and then give it to God. Only He can provide that thing we are seeking. Only God. Time moves with the swift transition, so much so, we must heal and move at the same time. The luxury of time is out of our control, and there is no time to waste. Time neither waits nor stops for anyone. We must learn to choose our battles, pray, and fight them moving. Nita thought herself to be a regimented soldier in the army of the Lord.

Forgiveness is easier with some issues; thus, Nita is yet in her process. There is a process for everything in life. We have held on to unforgiveness for so long that it has roots. We must pull that thing up by its root and kill it. Nevertheless, we must forgive to be free. We can't wholeheartedly serve God or others with the weight of unforgiveness. We can't operate with optimum performance holding grudges, hatred, and unforgiveness in our hearts.

Unforgiveness is relinquishing your control of self to the control of another person, place, or thing. The very presence of that person, place, or thing dictates how you will feel at that moment. We become puppets of our own emotions, at the mercy of others, all because we have not learned to forgive. We have yielded our power to the spirit of unforgiveness.

The phrase "I'm sorry" has lost its effectiveness because it is off the top of our heads and not genuine.
It means nothing when the term "I'm sorry" does not come from a change of heart and changed behavior. Repeat offenders have not made the transition, so the phrase has no significance. Without change, "sorry" is just another meaningless word. Apologies have no value if the posture remains the same.

Real sorrow is in the action.

Time offers no space or energy to hold on to negative and toxic feelings. Godly sorrow is in the change of behavior. Remember, our battle is not with flesh and blood. Our fight is not with each other. We must become effective in prayer and expedient with forgiveness, period.

CHAPTER 4

JOB TRAUMA AND ATTITUDE

Fast-forward.

Nita was blessed with an excellent job. The job paid her well, and she loved the work assigned to her. God blessed her with favor from the bosses. This favor extended from her immediate supervisor up to elected officials. Favor provided great fellowship with her coworkers. It's a blessing to work at a job and enjoy the work. It's such a reward to be compensated with favor in your profession. To be effective in the lives of others brings joy. This was the best-case scenario for Nita. A job may have brokenness as well. The brokenness can display itself through a boss or coworker. Brokenness is universal.

Support and professionalism were extended to Nita from all bosses except for one. Ms. May's unprofessional behavior became a learning tool for her. It is possible this boss learned to be nasty, controlling, and unprofessional to others from her former bosses. Nita recognized the same behavior as her former teacher. The teacher dismissed the students and showed indifference to them. Nita acknowledged indifference in her very own behavior. Many factors feed into our negative behavior. Insecurity can prompt people to be controlling and nasty, especially when they are challenged. The one boss was so unhappy that it seemed as if nothing could appease her. Her reports were prepared to exact specifications, they were on time, and yet, she complained. Nita came in early, worked through lunch, and stayed late, only to get more complaints. It takes an ardent effort to choose to be unhappy, every day.

Nita realized her attitude would only escalate the situation. She could surely match the boss's attitude if she so desired. Maybe the boss needed to meet the hands, but that would only give satisfaction to

Nita's flesh and not resolve the issue. That attitude would negate the effective goal she wished to achieve. She decided to flip the script and began to include this boss in her prayers. She was determined not to give away her joy, as she resolved she was working for God. Her mantra was not to allow anyone to interrupt her flow of money. She was most thankful for how God was growing and keeping her through this process of her life. Thank God for the grace to speak his Word even over oneself. Nita could honestly say if it had not been for the Lord, who was protecting both her and the boss, things could have certainly been different.

God provided Nita with the opportunity to have a candid conversation with the boss. The boss shared her dislike for Nita. The boss's dislike was due to the protection and support she felt Nita received from other bosses and colleagues.

Nita tried to convince her boss the support was due to her work ethic and nothing personal. The boss did not buy Nita's perspective but stuck to her narrative of favoritism and cronyism. Bosses should not mingle with staff on a personal level, this one boss felt. Nita was being punished because the bosses liked her. This boss did not realize Nita was a born leader, and God was making room for the assignment. The favor of God.

Nita asked the boss if there was a problem with her work, her attendance, or her customer service. She replied with a sarcastic no. "How do we proceed moving forward?" she asked, but there was no response. Nita left the boss's office convinced it was personal.

At the end of the day, Nita continued to give it all she had. Later, Ms. May was relieved of her duties. The moral of this story is that others can be jealous for no apparent reason. Some are so broken that their hatred is innate. This brokenness projects itself onto anyone in their path. Are we responsible for the perception others have of us? No, but we are responsible for how we respond. It was then Nita declared that when she became a boss, she would treat staff with the utmost respect. She would support them and coach them. She would not only train them but teach them to troubleshoot and resolve issues in her absence. She believed that one in authority should always criticize in private and praise in public.

Nita would be the opposite of her former boss. *How will you do this?* she asked herself. *God gave me gifts, and I will be a good steward of them.* She began by learning and mastering the job at hand. Nita would share her skills with the staff. She felt the key to success was to learn how, when, and what a boss required. Becoming an asset to your boss or company requires excellent listening skills. Understanding your job will yield success. Nita's targeted goal for her staff was to embrace the human side first and then address the expected goals.

Give good customer service to staff. Utilize people skills to show respect and compassion to staff. This motivates people to better apply themselves. If all else failed, staff would understand their job and receive appreciation for their efforts. Staff would know how it feels and what it means to give good customer service.

Like a boomerang, whatever you send out, comes back to you.

Your act of kindness signals that you value and appreciate the efforts of others. Yes, I am a boss. A God-fearing, professional, do-unto-others type of boss.

Kindness goes a long way.

Once again, what do we own, that God did not give to us? Nita learned that we take nothing to the grave with us. She once heard there would be no U-Haul truck following her hearse to the cemetery. In Nita's mind, that means to share, share, and be a good steward of those things God has given to us. Is it possible that jealousy has a role in our brokenness? Christians don't care to discuss jealousy. Jealousy is real. Insecurity is the other side of that coin. Jealousy and insecurity are first cousins. You can be jealous because of insecurity, and you can be insecure because of jealousy. Massage one, and both will live. Kill one, and both will die.

Sometimes, jealousy isn't only because of material things. People envy how others love you. People envy how you handle a situation. People envy your intelligence and how you make things happen. Jealousy is not limited to material things but includes intangibles such as the fruits of the spirit. If you are loving and kind, someone may think you are the weak link, not understanding you are the link that connects others. You are vulnerable to drawing others. Your influence will cause some to feel a certain way about you. Others are better in their nature than some of us are by practice. Nita thought her mom was easygoing because she was so kind. Yes, you are criticized for doing what the scripture demands you to do. Others have made it their life's goal to find fault in everyone but themselves. Every action is countered by a reaction. Jealousy unaddressed opens access to other ungodly spirits. It plants the seeds of bitterness and envy. What are we to do?

Acknowledging our brokenness is a good starting place. We are crushed in our spirit; life has gut-punched us, and we are all out of options. Acknowledgment opens the door to release and helps us to make the needed changes. Take off the masks and challenge yourself to discover God's purpose for your life. Lay aside every weight. Stay in the Word of God. Stay humbly at the altar, and no matter what, stay in the process. Believe prophetically in what the Word says and train yourself to wait on the Lord. In God's time, he will deliver us from ourselves.

Longevity on a job is an additional favor from God, where you learn the character of others. You learn work ethics, and coworkers become extended family. You get the opportunity to minister to others as you go through your individual life experiences. You get to meet all types of people from various backgrounds. One common denominator is working together towards the same goal. There are wise prayer warriors in those cubicles and broken and kind people in the cafeteria.

Some bosses are God-chasers. You learn to put the job, title, and career in their proper place: a means to an end, provision, and support.

The job is what you do and not who you are. If you are clear about what you do and who you are, you will excel.

Nita's goal is to take her best self wherever she goes, so she may grow.

This requires discernment. Discernment is not always fun to have because the spotlight is on you first. You cannot become angry when you are forced to address unpleasant things about yourself. It is a part of the process. Nita was unsure of her gift of discernment because she did not always have the correct response. Discernment gave her insight into the spirit of others. She realized when she paid close attention, people always showed who they are. You must know how to govern yourself with enlightenment.

Nita was the queen of attitude, her posture, and her speech all exuded attitude. If ever there was an attitude pageant, she would win, hands down. She could walk into a room, and her attitude would permeate the atmosphere, good or bad. She recognized it so well in others because she was consumed with attitude herself. She had an attitude for days and thus could spot it anywhere. The attitude she recognized in others simply mirrored her attitude. We are always able to recognize those things we are familiar with. You can possess all the skills and talent, only to negate it with a bad attitude. Brokenness taught Nita to call out the posture of a bad attitude within herself first and especially to the younger women. It's a proven fact.

Nita had to accept it for what it was and allow the Holy Spirit to transform her by renewing her mind. A real iron sharpens iron experience. A work in progress still. She realized that life is what you make it. You can be victorious or defeated. The choice is yours.

Nita liked people in general but had an annoyance with foolishness. If it did not make sense to her, it went into the foolish category. Nita's regimented home environment pushed her to strive for perfection in others as she did herself. This caused great anxiety. Here lies the problem. Nita had to learn the hard way there is no perfection in man. She did not find one scripture in the Bible that she penned or inspired. Neither will you. So, stop looking for perfection, and focus on the issues of the heart. Stop judging others when they don't move as you think they should. Our account before God is how and what we did, and not what others thought we should do.

The zeal of ignorance is the worst. Saul on the road to Damascus believed he was doing the right thing in persecuting Christians. Jesus took that same zeal and ignorance and transformed it for kingdom use. We also can believe that we are doing the right thing, only to find out we are wrong. I mean so wrong. Nita was overwhelmed with all the newfound information about herself, overwhelmed and excited about God's transformation within her.

Nita herself had operated with a zeal of ignorance. "There is no effectiveness in this posture," she said, as she desired to be effective in everything she did. Somewhere along the line, her wires crossed. She was spiritually broken. Broken and churched. Attitude is what Nita's older brother saw in her as a child and experienced from her as an adult. There were only two sides to Nita's personality, both on the opposite end of the spectrum. You either got a sweet Holy Spirit or, depending upon how you presented yourself, that carnal spirit. A carnal spirit allows people and outside forces to control the temperature of your emotions. Nita challenged herself not to allow outside forces to puppet her response. She was determined to stay on the effective side of the spectrum. The truth is her fleshly spirit was ever ready. She learned she must daily submit her flesh at the altar. She realized her battle was with her flesh.

Nita was taught to confess her sins, taught to humble herself and ask for forgiveness. She was taught confession is of no consequence without repentance. There must be a change.

John 1:9 says if I confess my sins, he is faithful and just to forgive me of my sins and to cleanse me from all unrighteousness (my attitude, my thoughts, my unforgiveness).

Heavenly Father, I thank you for all you have done and all you are doing in my life. I thank you for the revelation of your Word. I thank you for the healing power of your Word. I thank you for loving me while I was yet in my sins. I thank you for salvation. Hallelujah to your name. Thank you for revealing to me the things I need to change. Lord, I desire to be effective with the application of your Word.
I thank you for your love, your brand-new mercies, and your consideration for me. When I think of your goodness and mercy, it is mind-blowing. I must admit, I'm stuck there. I'm consumed, thinking about God's consideration of me and his compassion toward me. It has become the default praise that ushers me into worship. Your consideration of me makes my heart skip several beats. It is difficult to put into words just how good God is. "Hallelujah" just doesn't seem to be enough.

"Thank you" does not cover all the benefits, grace, and mercy that we receive each day. God has myriad mercies, so much so that David called it his multitude of tender mercies. God's mercy towards me is the driving force that keeps me in his Word.

Nita's praise and worship generate brand-new mercies and considerate compassion from God's love. It continues to knock Nita to her knees. The Lord considered her when she was reckless to others and herself. There was a time Nita was angry and hurt with God, mad that he allowed her mom and husband to die. She did not understand the connection between praying God's will be done in their lives and realizing his way was not her way. The spirit took Nita's mind to Job chapter 38, verse 4. God spoke to Job through a whirlwind. God asked Job a few questions, and Nita was convicted with the first question: Where were you when I laid the foundations of the earth? Checkmate. Lord, I was not to be found, as you did not need my help. Forgive me, Lord, for questioning and denying your sovereignty. Nita now stands in concert with Job in saying, "The Lord gives, and the Lord takes away. Blessed be the name of the Lord. Though he slays me yet; will I trust him."

Nita is forever full of thanks because life has shown her that situations could be so different. But God and his mercy, great is his mercy towards us.

In Psalm 51:8–12, David is expressing his repentance and remorse: "Make me hear joy and gladness; that the bones which thou have broken may rejoice. Hide thy face from my sins and blot out all mine iniquities. Purge me with hyssop and I shall be clean; wash me and I shall be whiter than snow. Create in me a clean heart Oh God and renew a right spirit within me. Cast me not away from thy presence and take not thy holy spirit from me. Restore unto me the joy of thy salvation; uphold me with thy free spirit."

Chronicles 7:14 jumped off the pages right before Nita, so she had to personalize it. "If My people, who are called by my name, should humble themselves and pray, seek my face, and turn from their wicked ways; then will I hear from heaven, will forgive their sins and heal the land?" Things look different when we make them personal.

People have no power or authority to give the validation Nita was seeking. We often place our joy, happiness, and peace in the hands of other broken people. We are all looking for the same things. It is an unreasonable expectation to look for validation from others. It is necessary to know who and whose you are.

I believe it was gospel artist John P. Kee who penned these words in a song: "Took my Faith away from men and then placed it in my savior's hand." Nobody can mold or hold us like you, Jesus.

CHAPTER 5

CHURCH TRAUMA AND BROKENNESS

Nita became more outspoken as she entered her teen years. In these years, her relationship with God became more personal. The Bible became her foundation, and she fell in love with the Word. The Bible housed all the answers, so Nita took to the Word like a duck to water. Word provided her with hope, comfort, and assurance. Nita found the Word of God ministered to her personally. Each of us comes away with our revelation, a revelation that feeds and encourages us. Nita found that to be amazing.

At this point, Nita asked the Lord to continue to show his purpose for her life, search her heart, and give direction. Nita asked the Lord to add effectiveness to her process.

Music was the kryptonite to Nita's thoughts and emotions. Her mom was a soloist. Singing and the appreciation of music were a given in her home. Each sibling shared their genre of music, creating a melting pot of musical enjoyment. Nita has fond memories of Ann and herself singing in the choir. Ann's first song she led in the youth choir was so powerful, and we were so proud of her. Music was the conduit for the Word. The Word came to life when placed to music in a song. Nita found her time singing in the choir to be very inspiring. Music ministered to her brokenness. Nita found the words to be powerful and full of hope. When you are down in your spirit, music gives the gift of hope. Hope offers life and the strength to continue. When life knocks your song out of you, humming works just as well.

Many a choir member was broken and churched. The mass choir sang, "Stand still and look up, God is going to show up, he is standing nigh; there's healing for your sorrow, healing for your pain, healing for your spirit, there's shelter from the rain." Does the spirit of the Word become more life-giving because one is broken? Yes, it does. For Nita, it did. Will the song minister first to the singer before it moves out to the congregation? Yes, it should. Our brokenness is crying out for the balm in Gilead to heal souls. Brokenness requires healing for the soul. Scripture says God inhabits the praises of his people. The Holy Spirit comes and ministers to each of us, individually and collectively. The musical chords soften the heartstrings to receive the words of a song. And yet we are broken.

Nita remembered her service as an usher and was proud to be a doorkeeper. She understood all the signs and moves at practice; however, her application in Sunday morning service was quite different. The usher board ministry taught Nita the goal was being effective, as opposed to being right. Nita was so thankful for this instruction, as she desired the Lord to see her as <u>effective.</u>

Being right does not offer help to those who are broken.
Being right does not offer help to us who are broken.

The Lord made room for the skills and talents he had placed inside Nita. She found herself in the finance ministry of the church, where she found more brokenness and a great lack of understanding. Within the finance ministry were trustees, deacons, and leaders of the church. There were finance officers who had a different understanding; they were not tithers. Not only were they not tithers, but some were against the Pastor. This baffled Nita. How can one be effective in the church and not support the man of God? Why are you there? Is it the image of looking pious with no substance? Oxymoron. Nita took notes for a later date.

Nita thought some to be more knowledgeable due to their age. Note: "Without wisdom, age is just a number." Is it possible these people were broken or was it simply a lack of knowledge? These were the thoughts and questions that raced through Nita's mind.

Nita prayed for effectiveness within this ministry; she asked God for his divine intervention and to lead her in the right direction. She was a young woman amongst a group of older men, signaling the opposition she would face.

It is difficult to penetrate archaic ideas that come backed by longevity and seniority. People are most eager to share how long they have been and how long they have done. Innovative ideas are looked upon as the enemy. Subliminally, women in positions of authority are not welcomed by all.

Finally, the finance meeting provided the opportunity for Nita to ask her questions and reveal her plans. How is one allowed to operate as a finance officer of the church and not pay the Lord's tithe? Who authorized one to count the church collections and not tithe? Why is there a side counting of collections? Why are collections taken to member homes? Where are the checks and balances? Nita's questions annoyed Deacon Owens and Deacon Thomas. Both deacons began to talk simultaneously as they spewed out their answers. The two deacons were not happy with Nita!

Deacons Owens and Thomas were the catalysts of discord within the church. They had controlled the flow of money and operations of the church for many years.

These men were allowed the same freedom within the church as Nita's younger brother was allowed at home.

"So many questions," retorted Deacon Owens. "Young lady, we have been doing this for years, and it's none of the Pastor's business what goes on in the Finance Department. How would he know who tithes? We do not report to him."

"Wait a minute," replied Nita. "None of the Pastor's business? This is unbelievable. Are you saying the finances of the church are none of the Pastor's business? Who do you report to, if not the Pastor?"

"My wife and I personally bought the church bus," said Deacon Owens.
"Yes, I see the record of that," Nita said. "My question is, how does this translate in your mind to the Lord's tithe?" Deacon Owens went on to say that he and his wife would fill in where they saw a need.
"There is a biblical command to tithe," said Nita. "With all due respect, your special offering was a beautiful blessing, but the church does not operate on the bartering system, and your offering does not give you the right to sow discord within the church. You have not addressed the question of tithing. I do believe the purchase of the church bus is an offering. Now my question is, can you make an offering without tithing? My question is rhetorical because it is obvious you did."

> Therefore, if thou bring thy gift to the altar, and there
> remember that thy brother hath ought against thee;
> Leave there thy gift before the altar and go thy way;
> first be reconciled to thy brother, and then come and
> offer thy gift. (Matthew 5:23–24)

"Tithing is from the Old Testament," Deacon Thomas said.

"Yes, you are correct; we can say tithing was voluntarily set up four hundred years before the law of Moses. Abraham gave a tithe to honor God."

Deacon Owens said, "We are no longer under the law but under grace."
"Correct," Nita said again. "Tithing was instituted before the law of Moses. Tithing is before the law. Jesus came to fulfill the law, which

includes those things under the law of Moses and the dispensation of grace. That covers both the Old and New Testaments.

"I'd also like to share 2 Corinthians 9:6–10: 'But this I say, He which soweth sparingly shall reap also sparingly; and he which soweth bountifully shall reap also bountifully. Every man according as he purposed in his heart, so let him give; not grudgingly, or of necessity: for God loveth a cheerful giver. And God will make all grace abound toward you; that ye, always having all sufficiency in all things, may abound to every good work.'"

Deacon Owens said, "So now you wish to turn the finance meeting into Bible study. I knew I would not like you. Exactly who do you think you are? I will not tolerate you and your newfound ideas."
My desire is to encourage us as believers to be on one accord. The problem with giving money because you have it to give it removes the humility of being a cheerful giver.
It leaves a bitter fragrance in the atmosphere. We must remain humble at all costs.
Never bragging or arrogant in giving. I applaud your gifts, but your understanding needs
to be adjusted if you will. "May I ask each of the deacons how you came to be a deacon?
Why are you a part of the finance ministry? Why are you here if you do not like the pastor?
I have reviewed the records and did not find where either of you pays the Lord's tithes,
so let me understand this. You don't support the pastor, and neither of you tithe. Help me to understand how you have access to the finances of the church?"

Deacon Thomas replied, "We were members before this Pastor was voted in. We have the authority to vote him out. I did not vote for him; he knows I never liked him. Again, young lady, whom do you think you are?"

Nita's mind drifted back to her days of creating mudpies. The words of Deacon Owens continued to spin around in her mind. *Who do I think I am?* Nita thought to herself. *I'm an entrepreneur since the age of eight, sirs.*

She created her own mud-pie business. Nita and Ann would go to the dirt pile in the
backyard to play each day. While playing, Nita thought she would make delicious mudpies from dirt, sand, and water. She would sell two mudpies for ten dollars. Every day, she would create her batch goal of one hundred, dry them in the sun, and package them in sandwich bags. She would decorate some with small pebbles. Nita believed in her business venture. Two mudpies for ten dollars would require a daily supply of fifty bags.

That would be five hundred dollars per day. Nita was extremely excited about her business. She had many thoughts about how to streamline her overhead and increase supply to meet the demand. Nita's dad began a hauling company after his honorable discharge from the military, so the entrepreneurial seed was innate. Nita's brother loved the mudpie business, probably because it kept his younger sisters out of his hair for hours.

One day, Ann said, "No one is going to buy any of this; I quit. I do not want to play with you anymore. You take the fun out of playing. Everything is about making money for you."

Nita hugged her sister and said, "Don't worry, lil' sis, I will always look out for you."
It was then Nita knew her sister did not understand the concept of business. She was sad because she saw her sister struggling in survival

mode. Yes, Nita knew it was dirt, sand, and water, but it birthed in her mind the principle of business, the idea of becoming a boss woman. Ann was looking at the tangible while Nita only saw the incredible, the invisible. She was working with a dozen men. Men were more knowledgeable and more powerful; even God deemed men as the head. God deemed man's position, so that settled it.

Nita thought, *While I cannot fight them physically, I can surely use the spirit of the Word to challenge their thinking.* It is no different from challenging her older brother's train of thought. Some laughed at the thought of Nita's mudpie business, but the mudpies ignited something within her. She loved her vivid imagination.

Nita was able to look beyond the mudpies and put everything in its place. She was amazed how her mind could drift off to wherever she willed it. I am an entrepreneur, Mr. Deacon Man, sir.

Deacon Owens asked, "You want to change the way we do things? I heard about you. Not while I'm here."

"For the record," Deacon Thomas added, "the entire church does not sit in on Finance Ministry Meetings."

Deacons Owens and Thomas were simultaneously responding to their emotions. Nita listened as they continued to speak, cutting each other off with emotional outbursts. At some point, Nita prayed they would move beyond their feelings and speak rationally. They each babbled while Nita continued to listen for clarity.

"Order," yelled one of the trustees. "Answer the questions one at a time; you cannot talk at the same time. Stop cutting her off! Please continue, Sister Nita."

"How did this minimal salary of the pastor come about?" Nita asked. "What are the thoughts behind such a low salary?"

"He receives enough to get along on," said Deacon Owens.

"Who decides the value of enough?" Nita asked. "A full-time pastor should be compensated by the Word of God and not our personal feelings. Should not the entire church be included on the overall items included within the Pastor's package? I wanted the entire congregation to be included in the new direction of the Finance Department. We need to reestablish clarity, honesty, and integrity."

"What package?" yelled Deacon Thomas. "I did not authorize a package."
Deacon Thomas, "this is one of the problems, you believe you have the power to authorize or not authorize. You may have operated in the past with this train of thought, but we will no longer operate in this manner. A new package will be agreed upon and presented to the Pastor by the financial officer. "Furthermore, the Pastor's salary is no longer governed by feelings, but by the word, as given in 1 Timothy 5:17–18: "Let the elders that rule well be counted worthy of double honor, especially they who labor in the word and doctrine. For the scripture saith, thou shalt not muzzle the ox that treads out the corn. And the laborer is worthy of his reward."

"Listen, my father, financed the very pews the congregation sits on," Deacon Thomas snapped.
"And this gives you the right to dictate if the pastor gets a package?" asked Nita.

"That's just personality," Deacon Owens said. "I don't see the need for all these questions. Some of us have been doing this since before you were born."

Nita did not know if the scriptures were appropriate for the current dialogue, but they got the attention of the trustees. She believed she could work with the trustees; she grew up with many brothers. After all, she brought much to the table: determination, skill, knowledge, wisdom, and attitude. Now that she had the attention of the trustees and congregation, she began to share her thoughts and plans for the finance ministry.

"Well, gentlemen, I have a clear picture of where each of you stands, and while not in agreement, I respect your opinions. I believe we should always be decent and in order. I have been directed to bring the finance ministry into compliance; we need to downsize and make much-needed changes. After reviewing the records and information provided to me, in addition to hearing your personal feelings, both of you are immediately removed from the finance ministry. Your presence is not conducive to kingdom building. It's not healthy to work within a ministry and not believe the Word of God or follow the man of God."

She added, "Deacons, your feelings about me are none of my business. However, you are free to take your objections of me up with the pastor." She then thanked Deacons Owens and Thomas for their service and asked for their keys to the finance room.

"I will not give my keys to anyone," Deacon Thomas said. "You don't have the power to remove me, young lady."
"That's quite all right," Nita responded. "I wanted to offer you the option of volunteering the keys. The locks are being changed as we speak. Nevertheless, per the church's bylaws and a majority vote, I can, and I have removed both of you from the finance ministry. My definition of removal is as follows: no access to church bank accounts, no access to the finance room, and your names will be removed from all signatory platforms. No access to any financial items or issues concerning this church."
Nita suggested Deacons Owens and Thomas come into agreement with the Pastor before joining another ministry within the church.

What stood out in Nita's mind was the deacons did not see anything wrong with their train of thought or their controlling spirits.

Turned out there were more disgruntled members who did not like the Pastor. Deacon Owens and Deacon Thomas, along with some of the charter members, angrily threatened to leave the meeting. The entire congregation was in an uproar, and it took the trustees several minutes to bring the meeting back to order.
Nita thought to herself, *let them go.*

It had to be the Holy Spirit, she thought. *Not so bad. The disgruntled members revealed themselves at the meeting. It's a good thing to know who and what you are up against. Once the computers and software are set up, we can eliminate night drops. Wow,* Nita thought. *Decent and in order.*

Decent and in order blessed the church, neighborhood outreach programs, missionary ministries, scholarship fund, tutors for the children, and both singles and senior's ministry. Ministries were spiritually growing. Membership even increased by 10 percent. *Regimented thinking works when used properly,* Nita thought. *Thanks, Dad.*

This ministry's meeting is always open to the entire congregation for many reasons, including transparency, clarity, and accountability. Nita outlined the changes for the approval of the officers and trustees. The pastor's calendar does not permit him time to sit in on every meeting; moving forward, he must be updated on the church's financial standing. The finance ministry now requires dual signatures.

A Pastor's calling first and foremost is the Word of God. Can you imagine shepherding spiritual and carnal members every day? Imagine placing the needs of these members before your own family, rude, disrespectful members who are governed by their carnality. Imagine sacrificing your family's needs for the members of the church, praying and counseling members with various needs, interacting with difficult members, and members with their agenda. These are some of the responsibilities tasked to a pastor. Does not sound alluring or fancy. Neither does the job offer many options. I'm sure there will be times when we individually and collectively may disagree with a decision of a pastor. During these times, we must tell ourselves the pastor was called and anointed to do the job. God did not require the pastor to consult us or get our approval. Once I remind myself of that fact, I fall back into my place.

God bless the pastor, thought Nita; *the deacons needed the hands and then some Holy Oil as well.*

Nita directed the attention of the officers and trustees to the handouts she gave them and then began speaking.

"The following changes are a witness to our integrity. The church is a spiritual organism and a structured organization. The organizational piece requires the assistance and support of the body of members associated with the said church. Lack of structure feeds into those negative ideas many currently have of the church and how the church handles money."

Nita began to explain the immediate changes within the finance ministry.

The overall changes are as follows and effective immediately:

- Package for the pastor, inclusive of retirement (TBD). His current salary is short of an honorarium.
- Deacon Owens and Deacon Thomas are no longer part of the Finance Ministry. (They no longer have access to any church bank accounts or financial records.) let the records show.
- Every beliver should be a tither (time, talent, and tenth).
- All collections will come directly to the finance room (honesty; no more side-counting).
- Checks and balances (integrity; trustees and finance clerks to be used as counters).
- Multiple avenues to tithe are now available, including envelopes and cash apps.
- Trustees assigned to finance clerks (security for night drops to the bank).
- Church funds and church records no longer go to members' homes (honesty).

Nita concluded, "All present members are asked to sign the given handout as approval of the information discussed tonight. Your cooperation is greatly appreciated. Thank each of you for coming out to be a part of this meeting."
The trustees closed the meeting with prayer.

Deacons Owens and Thomas promised to fight Nita tooth and nail. Nita expected nothing less. Every subsequent Sunday brought a new surprise or dilemma.
The deacons allowed their emotions to control their logic. You are unstoppable when operating within the will of God. The deacons

had yet to learn it was God orchestrating the changes; Nita was only the conduit. God gave Nita the gift of administration and the vision to accomplish the task.

Kingdom building was at its best until brokenness again reared its head. Could it be the toxicity of the two deacons and the disgruntled members spread to the ministries or possibly to new members? Toxicity, like wildfire, only takes one member to fan the flames.

Once again, Nita was forced to realize the spirit of brokenness needed to be addressed. Many of us actively fellowship and utilize our time, talent, and tenth to promote the kingdom, yet we are broken.

Love the Lord with all our hearts and continue to mask our brokenness. Life happens to us all. Life is an equal opportunist, to the prominent, the less fortunate, the educated, and even the Pastors. Life happens to us all. *Even I* thought Nita. She took everything she witnessed in others and continuously examined herself. She knew she was a work in progress. We never totally arrive here on earth, so it is a process. Release from brokenness requires us to be honest with ourselves in admitting we are broken, acknowledging we need a personal makeover and God's divine intervention. Nita realized that if God could use her, the sky was the limit for anyone. In looking back over her life, Nita realized God loved her. From embryo to this present day, brand-new mercies, and more grace.

God has been protecting Nita from dangers seen and unseen. God's grace and mercy are teaching her to forgive. He had a plan and a purpose for her life. She could not get out of God's plan if she wanted to. Neither can you.

Nita noticed there was a lack of people skills within the congregation. Lack of skills in ministering to the home base impacted their evangelism. Members offered poor customer service to each other.

Younger members were disrespectful to older members. The middle-aged members had not fully solidified their footing, which caused them to be deceitful and messy. Seasoned members stepped out of their place of respect, to be disrespected. Carnal and spiritual all churched together.

CHAPTER 6

HAVE MERCY ON US OH, GOD

Teamwork was nonexistent. Same goals with different agendas? There was no allegiance or unity. Poor customer service in the house equals poor customer service out of the house. This was a direct hit on evangelism and discipleship. Something was amiss. Christians must remember the enemy operates within territories. The territory of cliques, controlling spirits, jealousy, and insecurity are all portals we open to allow the enemy a stronghold. Where the work of the flesh is practiced, a strongman accompanies because territories and regions are where the devil operates.

Good customer service says I am prepared to offer you the best I can give. Yes, you may be irritating, nasty, and impatient; and I will not take it personally.
Given the opportunity, I will help you resolve your issue. Nita learned in service with the IRS to address the caller by listening with understanding to come to a resolution. It works. Jesus meets us at our point of need, exactly where we are, and with practice, we can meet and minister to others.

Exodus 20:12 says, "Honor thy father and thy mother: that thy days may be long upon the land which the LORD thy God giveth thee." Once again, charity begins at home. When we train our children to observe this command, they will reap the promise. When we train our children to hide the Word in their hearts so they may not sin against God, the hedge of protection is not broken. The scripture tells us to train a child, and although they may depart, they will return to their original training, if the Lord is willing.
Our biggest investment is one another.

Our efforts to hurt or embarrass others reflect the condition of our hearts, and like a boomerang, it comes back to hurt us. If we believe the body is one with many members, why do we not embrace all members? If my ears decide they want to be my eyes, it does not change their given assignment to hear.

Nita desired to become her best self. She needed to solidify who she was and understand her position to the best of her ability. There was no shame coming from Nita, as she learned early in life to laugh at herself. Thank God for brothers.

Nita was not looking to find these broken members, but they continued to show themselves. Sad, hurt, and broken. Is it possible Nita's brokenness allowed them to come out of hiding? Her best work came through her brokenness.

Was it possible the broken members could see her growth? Nita's brokenness allowed her to be more vulnerable and accessible. She was a listener and always tried to embrace the members. She was an advocate for the ostracized and the misunderstood.

No matter what the cause, Nita was more than ready to stand to their defense with support. This was a part of her assignment, even in her process of development.

Although Nita was open to the many members who shared their issues with her, she would tell them God is the only one who can validate and heal us. God is the only source of validation, yet we continue to seek validation from other broken people. We continue to seek validation from our jobs, titles, and money. Nita learned that our jobs and titles are the avenues given by God to support ourselves, our ministry, and others in need.

Nita remembered time money was her validation: borderline idol. Our Pastor is teaching us how to build solid. 1 Corinthians 10:31 says whether we eat or drink, whatsoever we do, do it all to the glory of God. Upon placing God back as the headliner, even our finances fall into place.

Nita had played God in the lives of her family. She was the enabler, always attempting to push others to what she deemed a better position in life for them, only to find the push needed to be twofold. Nita's heart's desire was for her children, grandchildren, and family members to depend upon God. We must encourage our children to trust God. He alone is the source. We must remove ourselves and step out of the way so God can be exalted. Nita remembered trusting God to make a way, and he did. We must trust God, period. God has never failed Nita to this day.

Anyone or anything we use to replace God fails. God had to bring Nita into the right understanding of money. He chastens those he loves. He did not remove money from Nita but minimized her access to it. She had to learn to trust God in all things; money could not be a hindrance to her assignment. It was uncomfortable, but Nita understood and was thankful that God had compassion for her brokenness.

Brokenness helps us to see our part; the Holy Spirit provides direction through our brokenness. It was within Nita's brokenness God was still showing himself as a provider and healer, still molding that seed he placed in little Nita. Is brokenness the place where God does his best work? Pastor Hunter says things happen on purpose for a purpose.

Psalm 51:17 says, "The sacrifices of God are a broken spirit: a broken and a contrite heart, O God, thou wilt not despise."

We know all the Christian jargon and all the biblical clichés, yet we are not as effective as we should be. We know all the signs, rules, and positions just as the usher; however, our application is off. Church jargon and clichés are not the answer when in a state of brokenness.

Nita can remember on many a Sunday sitting in church, heart bleeding, so heavy in her spirit and mute, unable to put on the garment of praise due to the heaviness of being broken. Now, due to the consistency of prayer and the Word, the sanctuary is saturated with the presence of God. The atmosphere is welcoming as you enter his gates with thanksgiving and into his courts with praise. God's aroma entices and his presence overwhelms.

There is a spirit of expectation placed upon believers. A worldly standard is placed upon believers that do not allow space to be human. I believe when Believers opt to adhere to anything other than the Word of God, it throws the PH balance of our spirit off. Christians waste time and effort in attempting to prove, "Yes, I'm a Christian; see my credentials. Yes, look at my work." We are Christians by our show of love. More importantly, <u>we are human and not perfect</u>.

We harm ourselves and our witnesses by attempting to give an image of being something we are not.
We harm ourselves and our witnesses trying to promote this false image of how pious we believe ourselves to be. Yes, Christian believers should be saved and sanctified,
but even that does not make us perfect. We are quick to point out the flaws of others and excuse ourselves for those same flaws.
We all have broken issues and addictions of some kind. Jesus the peacemaker said it best: "Let he who is without sin cast the first stone." John 8:7b(KJV)You are supposed to be Christians some say" Does that not apply to you as well?

Unbelievers need to see our behavior agree with our spoken words. Our Christ-like behavior attracts them to hear and desire the Word of God.

<u>We often try to convince other broken people that we are worthy of their broken approval.</u>

Brokenness reveals our hypocrisy towards each other. We do not study to show ourselves approved because Sister Jane is teaching. We do not like a member because of something said by another member. Do we not have minds of our own? Do not cheat yourself out of the blessings God has for you. Whom are you serving?

We cannot afford to miss the message by focusing on the messenger. Messengers must keep in mind their assignment is to plant or water. Only God can give the increase. Will you refuse your paycheck because it came by mail and was not direct deposited? No, I do not believe you would. Do not miss a life-saving Word because you are operating with a false narrative. Sit on those emotions. Other believers are merely using what God has given them. We all should do the same. Image can never produce substance.

Emotions have their place, but emotions are not the place. When emotions do not reflect the fruits of the spirit, they are out of place.

There should be no competition among believers. What God has for you is for you. Most of our hypocrisy with each other is rooted in jealousy and competition. Everyone has been blessed with an area of expertise. Our individuality will cause us to address a task differently. This does not make one right or wrong; it speaks to the individual. Our spiritual gifts were given to enhance and support, not war with each other. Pastor Keion Henderson said *if we stop coming to church for people, then we will not leave the church because of people. We must stop making God pay or hold God accountable for something people said or did.*

> Out of the depths have I cried unto thee, O Lord,
> hear my voice: let thine ear be attentive to the voice
> of my supplication. (Psalm 130:1–2)

John 12:43 says they loved human praise more than praise from God. We should focus on pleasing God rather than people. Off with the mask of an image.

> I am the true vine, and my father is the husbandman. Every branch in me that bears no fruit he taketh away: and every branch that bears fruit, he purges it, that it may bring forth more fruit. Now ye are clean through the word which I have spoken unto you. (John 15:1)

Get connected, and stay connected, because the Word is essential.

Scripture advises us not to give place to the devil, to allow him to torture us with our vain imaginations. Debating the Word of God weakens our witness to others. The Bible says you have the choice to believe or not. My dad said what he meant and meant what he said, and we, his children, respected him. My dad's track record was our proof. If there was a problem, we went to him for answers. Dad taught his children to fight, and we did it exceptionally well in the flesh. Our mother taught us how to fight in the spirit, thus the Word of God was deposited early in our lives. When we needed that special love or word of encouragement, we went to our mother. She operated through the fruits of the spirit. Each of our parents provided wisdom from opposite sides of the spectrum. Nita did not understand how her mom came to be so peaceful, quiet, and tranquil. All her answers were soft and kind.

Nita did not fully understand her mother's posture until she was well up in age. Her Mom's posture was the best posture one could have. When you can hold your peace during turmoil, you are not weak but strong.

2 Corinthians 12:9 tells us that God's grace is sufficient for us; for God's strength is made perfect in our weakness.

Our challenge as children and now adults is to find the balance. Take what we need from each parent, apply it, and grow. We all need spiritual balance and faith in the Word and through the Word. The prayer of faith, the faith of prayer, all lead us to the Word. Nita continues to strive for balance.

God is so good, patient, and loving toward us. His grace and mercy are exceeding and abundantly beyond anything we could ask or even imagine. I do not believe it is malicious, but we often take his goodness for granted. It is mind-blowing to have the doctors pronounce a sentence of death over a loved one's life, and God intervenes, confuses the doctors, and says live a little longer on this side. God is a keeper to those of us who keep him. His record is matchless with universal credibility. He is in a league all by himself. How about we are all sinners, saved by grace? God's grace and mercy.

Romans 8:1 tells us there is therefore now no condemnation to them who are in Christ Jesus, who walk not after the flesh, but after the spirit.

Christ was human and divine. Humans are not.

Christ took on our sins. It is the work of the enemy, or we who bring about doubt and question what God has done in the lives of his people. Only God has the answer for what we seek.

Nita's cousin Erica experienced some horrific storms in life. Horrible and unimaginable, devastating to the point where it paralyzed her mind and heart. Nita often wondered if the brokenness of the relative's life experiences was fueled by the constant negativity she spewed.

Nita believed Erica tortured herself with her very own words. The constant regurgitation, over and over and over. We often torture ourselves with our own negative and toxic thoughts.

Erica shared every negative event with anyone who would listen. She was unable to break free. The truth of the matter, her story was as real as her pain. I mean, real, real, real. I empathized and sympathized with her emotions, but I wondered if she could ever be free in her mind and spirit. I can only imagine the torture of reliving the events in her mind. Each time Nita would hear the stories, it triggered anxiety and headaches. Trauma will keep you in perpetual agony until you release it and are free.

At what point do we release, forgive, and try to move on with our lives? At what point do we realize the negativity is now airborne, transferring to all who come in contact? It has been said that unforgiveness is like drinking poison and waiting for the other person to die. I would imagine unforgiveness is an ingredient of insanity.

Holding on to unforgiveness, hurt, and anger gives the enemy permission to torture us with our thoughts and emotions. Holding on to toxic emotions plays a vital role in our physical and mental health. We become our own worst enemies.

Unforgiveness is passed on to our children, who mimic our behavior. Our disrespect for our parents permits our children to be disrespectful to us. It's a vicious cycle. Remember, we are extensions of our socialization. Unforgiveness allows one to live with a victim mentality: me, me, me. Unforgiveness releases itself physically, mentally, and emotionally. We experience sickness and disease because we hold on to the hurt and pain. The hurt and pain then become putrid and begin to poison our bloodstream. It must release itself in some way.

Nita's literal, visual imagination pictured unforgiveness as one walking around wearing two fur coats, a fur hat, gloves, and boots in 110 degrees of heat. The weight of unforgiveness is overwhelming. Nita realized through her cousin Erica that some childhood trauma is like wearing a cement overcoat every day: paralyzed and unable to move.

Trauma and some of our hurts are too much for us to manage or overcome, so we tap out. Deep in our spirit, we know we need a Word, so we enter the sanctuary in a zombie-like manner, hoping a Word would fall on us, praying someone would care enough to see us and address our pain. Scripture says to cast our cares upon God for he cares for us.

Broken Christians are often unable to ask for help due to the weight of guilt they carry. Broken Christians hope to avoid the judgment of other broken Christians. Most people still don't realize they are also broken. We continue to wear our masks, our pre-pandemic masks, our blind-leading-the-blind masks. Once you can admit you are broken, the spiritual portal is opened, and you are granted access to see yourself and realign yourself with God's purpose.
All because of the Word. Pain awakens us to focus on our mental and spiritual condition.

Pastor Hunter gave a visual sermon titled "It Is Time to Unpack." Matthew 11:28–30. The weight of carrying dead and nonproductive issues in our hearts every day hinders our spiritual growth. Pastor's visual showed
us how we carry these issues with us everywhere we go.

Believers today mainly see the outside appearance and are too pious to address the pain of brokenness. We are only concerned with appearance and not reality. We can be a hot minute away from homelessness, and yet we continue to keep the pious image going. We cannot be helped if we do not admit we need help. We cannot be healed until we admit we are broken.

Is there any wonder why some do not attend church and others do not fellowship? Some do not even believe in God. Due to our brokenness, others cannot see the God in us, and thus they continue to be broken. We each have unknowingly contributed to the brokenness of others through our brokenness.

Hurt people do hurt people, especially in church. Brokenness, added to the criticism, can never give the needed deliverance.

Pastor Hunter said anyone or anything other than God is not dependable. He is our protection and our refuge. We must learn to press the faith button instead of the panic button. It is difficult to serve God with our hearts and minds all over the place. Our hearts and minds need to be _in_ one accord, _with_ one accord.

The pandemic forced us to focus more on prayer and the Word and forced us to look at ourselves, our way of doing things, and their alignment with the Word of God. We came to remember our ways were not his ways and our thoughts were not his thoughts. The pastor was correct; we must push our faith button several times a day or live in panic mode. We must focus, stay prayerful, and stay in the Word. Remember, our weapons of warfare are mighty in God to the pulling down of strongholds.

Brokenness is like going to the gas station only to find there is no fuel in the pumps or going to Costco or Walmart and there are no paper towels on the shelves. Paper towels were never so important until the pandemic. We took for granted these items would always be available in stores; this pandemic proved us wrong. The pandemic also caused us to look internally at ourselves.
Thus, we can no longer minimize the Word or take it for granted. We must seize the moment and get our study on.

Criticism only causes broken people to shut down and create another mask. The cycle continues, and we are still broken. My disclaimer is, I do not believe the intent of the following statement is malicious, but the use of the word in this context is not effective but is an offensive and inappropriate cliché. "If" when used in a certain context negates or gives off a negative implication, such as "If the Lord has done anything for you." It is used to indicate suppositions or hypothetical conditions that involve doubt or uncertainty. Used in this context, it negates God's authority. "If he healed you," says, did he heal you? "If he saved you," asks, did he save you? Used in this context, it does not encourage or motivate; it comes across as a negative attack. The other side of it yells to the listener, "I need you to behave a certain way so I can validate your Christianity." Listeners and believers will always shut down when feeling attacked.

Use Your Freedom for God's Glory (Corinthians 10:23, 31)

"All things are allowed," you say. But not all things are good. All things are allowed. But some things don't help anyone.

if you eat, or if you drink, or if you do anything, do it for the glory of God.

I am not trying to do what is good for me. I am trying to do what is good for other people so they can be saved. It points back to one planting the Word, one watering the Word, and God giving the increase. In our effort to be effective, our words should always embrace, attract, or even woo others to Christ. When the line of communication is a gray area, we may need to consider a more effective way to phrase our cliché.

> And Jesus being full of the Holy Ghost returned from
> Jordan, and was led by the Spirit into the wilderness,
> Being forty days tempted by the devil. In those days
> he [Jesus] did eat nothing: and when [the forty days]
> were ended, he afterward hungered.

And the devil said unto him [if] thou be the Son of God, command this stone to be made bread. [Satan knew the negative implication of the word *if* when used out of context. It questioned Jesus's relationship with God.]

But Jesus answered him, saying, It is written, That man shall not live by bread alone, but by every word of God. [Notice how Jesus did not even address the "if thou be the Son of God" part.] (Luke 4:1-4)

We can do nothing without God, and for that, he is worthy to be praised. There are several things we must unlearn to become more effective. Even with the best intentions, we may offend. We must get rid of this notion that Christians need to prove something to us for credibility or acceptance.

We must use different postures to be effective, a posture that does not offend others or question the deity of God. A more welcoming word would yield a pleasant result. *I believe when we keep Jesus as the headliner, and not ourselves or how we feel, others will join in concert, however, slow they may be. Let us not forget we have no gift of salvation to give to anyone. Remember, we have no heaven or hell to give to anyone, not even ourselves. Let us become Christians of Substance rather than selling an image.*

As the deacons asked Nita, "Who does she think she is?" The suggestion that Christians must move a certain way to satisfy us is utterly preposterous. Let's come to our senses and stop wasting time with foolery. We shall be known by our love. Everyone has the right to disagree or have their version, which I wholeheartedly respect. However, I do adamantly believe our presentation can help us win souls or cost us to lose souls.

People are hurting right in our midst, yet we continue with our pomp and circumstance. We wear our indifference to church without regard because we know another broken person will justify that is just how they are.

Stop it; people would be better if you addressed the brokenness as opposed to justifying it. We cannot expect better from others until we demand better from ourselves. We are all in this, together and broken.

One of our ministers preached a sermon titled "Wounded Worshiper," referencing Acts 16:16–34. This sermon was so in tune with brokenness. It was another confirmation of the Word agreeing with itself. I am convinced brokenness is that place where our spirits were crushed; brokenness is the best posture of humility. It is the place where God can mold us for service. When we are weak, God is strong.

Minister Portia made a statement, and I quote, "Paul and Silas were clear about their assignment." She went on to tell us they had been stripped, dragged, and beaten, placed in stocks within the depths of the prison. Paul and Silas decided their situation deserved praise and worship: wounded and yet worshipping.
Broken and still praising God, clear on what would get God's attention. Clear about their purpose; even the prison guards and their families came to receive salvation, all because God was the headliner. The focus was on God. Remember, if I (God) be lifted, I (God) will draw. To push past your heartaches and disappointments, and worship in your brokenness is the ultimate contrite heart.

Nita remembered another minister who said, "Not to allow the *inner me* to become the *enemy.*" Nita thought to herself, brokenness is our battle between the inner me and the enemy. We often torture ourselves with our very own toxic thoughts. Once thoughts take root, they manifest themselves in our behavior. We then get in our way. The slippery slope is tricky because <u>we cannot see what we will not address</u>. We are unable to heal those areas we will not admit are broken.

On another occasion, Minister Lee discussed the words "thank you" and "grateful." once again confirming the word itself in the spirit. Each one spoke to something Nita was writing. We often say "Thank you" so much without meaning until it loses its power. Minister Lee said this is the place where our gratitude propels us into worship. Gratitude and gratefulness.

We praise God for who he is and thank him for all he has done. Minister Lee's words were so clear. <u>Hebrews 11:6 says, without faith it is impossible to please him.</u> Him who? Who is he to you? It is impossible to please someone you don't even know. How can one have faith in someone or something they have never tried?
God rewards those who personally know him, intentionally seek him, and wholeheartedly believe that he exists to bless them. Let us keep it real; unbelievers will not express faith or seek out someone they don't believe in or trust. We have the God-given sense to seek our God who specializes in results, results like salvation and healing. Amen.

You cannot say "Thank you" without being grateful; "thank you" is how we express our gratitude. We show our gratitude through audible praise of thank you, bless you, we love and adore you. Nita later realized the exhortations were more affirmations and confirmations of the Word. Nita would ask God a question, and the next day or Sunday's sermon yielded the answer. Nita realized the

Word of God supports the Holy Spirit, and the Holy Spirit supports the Word of God. Like the opposite sides of the same coin. Even the Word of God works together for our good. So amazing.

Nita is thankful to be a student of the Word.

CHAPTER 7

MASTER OF BROKENNESS

What is the difference between a teacher and a trainer? Why was Jesus called the Master Teacher? What is a parable?

A teacher shares information with the objective of understanding for application.
Information + understanding = application.

A trainer shares a process or procedure to reach a targeted goal.
Process + procedure = targeted goal.

Jesus used parables or stories, including time-relevant examples, for moral lessons. A parable is a simple story used to illustrate a moral or spiritual lesson, like Aesop's fable, only Jesus is the narrator. Jesus wanted his listeners to fully understand his message and his teachings; he used those things about everyday life.

As the Master Teacher, Jesus set the foundation and delivered the facts of information. This manner of teaching awed his listeners and inspired them to change. Jesus taught and trained simultaneously. He combined both teaching and training, infused with his divinity. People came away wanting more because Jesus met them where they were physically, emotionally, socially, and spiritually. Jesus taught, trained, and evangelized under the auspices of the Holy Spirit, and thus he is the Master Teacher.

Jesus shared many parables, and thus the crowds grew and grew. God said, let there be, and so it was. Words are backed up with actions. Needs were supplied, people healed, delivered, and set free by his words. Talking about keeping it 100, Jesus's actions created the meaning of the Great Commission: evangelism.

(Psalm 150:6 "Let everything that has breath, praise the Lord!"). There is breath in an earthquake displaying the great power of God; there is breath in the sun displaying the glory of God. Likewise, we have the breath of life already in us, and we can use that same breath to praise God for his goodness.
We must strive to be effective in our deportment and thus witness the manifestation of real change.

Another morning on the prayer line, Minister Tamara took us to Luke 8:27–37. Jesus and his disciples arrive in Gentile territory. Although the Gentiles were not yet ready to invite Jesus into their midst, they could not ignore the change in the man with the legion of demons.

> When Jesus went forth to land, there he met a certain man from the city who had devils for a long time and wore no clothes, the man did not live in any house but in the tombs.

> When he saw Jesus; he cried out and fell before him, and with a loud voice said, "What have I to do with thee Jesus, thou Son of the highest God? I beg of you, not to torment me."

> For he [Jesus] had commanded the unclean spirit to come out of the man. For oftentimes it had caught him: and he was kept bound with chains and in

fetters, and he broke the bonds and was driven of the devil into the wilderness.

And Jesus asked him, saying, "What is thy name?" And the man said, "Legion" because many devils were entered into him. [To understand the idea of a legion, the Roman soldiers' legion equaled six thousand. This man had a minimum of six thousand demons in him. The demons not only controlled but took over his identity and thus Legion was his name.] And they besought him that he would not command them to go out into the deep. And our Lord acted on the principle of not casting that which was holy to dogs, nor pearls before men whose moral character tended to become like that of their swine.
And there was a herd of many swine feeding on the mountain: and they besought him that he would suffer them to enter them. And he suffered them.
Then went the devils out of the man and entered the swine: and the herd ran violently down a steep place into the lake and were choked.
When they that fed them saw what was done, they fled, and went and told it in the city and the country.

Then they went out to see what was done; and came to Jesus, and found the man, out of whom the devils were departed, <u>sitting at the feet of Jesus, clothed, and in his </u>right mind: and they were afraid.

They also which saw it told them by what means the man possessed of the devils was healed.

Nita found this last verse interesting. It appears our brokenness brings comfort to some and discomfort to others. *Healing can be offensive to people who benefited from your brokenness. What? Yes, some will be angry and annoyed when you get healed and delivered.*

Others see our brokenness as normal, not requiring a need for healing or change. The multitude of the country of the Gadarenes was very comfortable and accustomed to the man with his legion of demons. They had no regard for him until the demons were driven from the man into the herd of swine. They knew his behavior, knew his broken process, and the man's process was a part of their norm. How dare Jesus tamper with their peace, their money, and their familiarity with the man's legion of demons? The people of the town hated Jesus for disturbing their daily routine. Satan had claimed this region as his territory. Brokenness became a source of fear only when the man was healed. The man cried out for help to the fear of others.

What are you thinking, Nita? Familiarity does bring contempt. The healing process of our brokenness will cause some to distance themselves because we all like to remember people <u>when</u>. I knew him <u>when</u> he was on drugs. I knew him <u>when</u> he was out of his mind. I remember seeing him walking down Cole Street naked and talking to himself. Chile, you cannot think <u>when</u> he comes around; he will steal your thoughts. He used to steal so much you had to pretend you were invisible. I remember <u>when</u> she was a prostitute. Girl, she was a hot mess. I mean she was torn up. We are most comfortable with the <u>"before Christ" of people</u>. We challenge and place doubt if there was any change at all.

We desire to keep everyone inside the <u>limited box of our minds</u> <u>because we fear</u> growth. Growth causes us to become uncomfortable. Growth requires us to change. Misery loves company, and because I am broken, I need you to remain broken. I liked you better when you were broken; I could dictate your next move based on my previous experience with you. The multitude's hidden agenda cared more about the pigs than the value of the man's soul.

One of life's traps is to value things more than people.

"Then the whole multitude of the country of the Gadarenes surrounded him [Jesus] to depart from them; for they were taken with great fear as his presence disturbed their routine" (Luke 8:37).

"The Spirit of the Lord is upon me because he hath anointed me to preach the gospel to the poor; he hath sent me to heal the brokenhearted, to preach deliverance to the captives, recovering of sight to the blind, to set at liberty them that are crushed" (Luke 4:18). God is Master over brokenness.

The Prodigal Son is a familiar story that speaks to brokenness, manifested as unforgiveness, arrogance, and compassion. Nita paraphrased the narrative.

Before we get into the story, let's go back to verse 1 and set the scene. Luke 15:1–10 starts with the publicans (tax collectors) and sinners coming close to hear what Jesus had to say. The murmuring Pharisees and scribes also came, complaining that he received sinners and ate with them. Jesus then began to give them milk (they were not yet ready for meat). Which of you who has one hundred sheep and loses one will not leave the ninety-nine to go and find the lost one? Would you not rejoice over finding the lost sheep and go rejoicing to your friends and say I have found my lost sheep? Better yet, if a woman has ten pieces of silver and loses one, will she not light a candle, sweep the house, and look until she has found it? When she finds it, will she not rejoice? This rejoicing is likewise in heaven over one sinner who repents, and there is joy in the presence of the angels of God over one sinner who repents. Then Jesus dropped the nugget of the Prodigal Son.

Jesus spoke this parable to the scribes and Pharisees who always gathered to critique him:

A certain man had two sons.

The younger son asked his father to give him the amount he would inherit, and the father gave him his portion of the estate.

Not many days after, the younger son packed up his belongings and left, headed for an unfamiliar place, and began to party. He made choices that prematurely exposed him to a lifestyle of poverty.

After he found himself broke, there was a famine and he was hungry to the point of starvation.

He went and attached himself to a citizen of that far country and the citizen sent him into his fields to feed the pigs.

And he was happy to fill his belly with the same husks the pigs ate because no man gave him food.

When <u>he came to his senses</u>, he reasoned with himself and said, my father's servants have more than enough food and I perish.

I will get up and go to my father and confess that I have sinned against heaven and him; I'm not worthy to be your son and ask to be hired as a servant.
He arose and went to his father, but his father saw him long before he got to him, his father's compassion caused him to run to meet his son, he fell on the son's neck and kissed him.

And the son said unto him, Father I have sinned against heaven and in thy sight and am no more worthy to be called thy son. [When we confess our sins …]

But the father said to his servants, bring forth the best robe, and put it on him; and put a ring on his hand, and shoes on his feet. [God is faithful and just to forgive us and cleanse us from all unrighteousness.] God's compassion is so great toward us.

And bring the fatted calf, and kill it, and let us eat and be merry.

For my son was dead and is alive again; he was lost and is found. And they began to be merry.

Now the elder son was in the field: as he approached, he heard music and dancing.

And he called one of the servants to ask what these things meant.

And the servant said, your brother has returned home, and your father has killed a fatted calf because he is safe and sound.

And the elder brother was angry and would not go in the house, so his father came out to inquire about him.

And he answered his father; All these years, I have served thee, neither have I disobeyed thee. Yet you have never given me even a kid that I might make merry with my friends.

But as soon as your son comes back after he has wasted all your money and devoured himself with prostitutes, you kill a fatted calf for him.

And he said unto him, son you have always been with me. All I have is yours. You could throw a banquet for yourself at any time.

It is a good thing that we make merry and be glad: for your brother was dead in his sins and is alive again, he was lost and is now found. (Luke 15:11)

Initially, one would think of the younger brother as the carnal one because he wanted his inheritance to go out on his own. The younger brother was exposed to some things he was not prepared for. He suffered the consequences of his decisions.
What Nita loved about the story is that he came to his senses.

Not everyone gets the opportunity to come back from a bad decision.

Not everyone is blessed to experience God's healing and live to tell it. Hallelujah.

The younger son came to himself, reasoned with himself, and took himself back to his father, who was waiting with so much love and compassion to bind the brokenness of his son. Forgiveness at its best. The father went on to address the indifference of the elder son, who was in the house and yet broken. In the house and envious. In the house and holding grudges. In the house but refusing to fellowship. In the house and angry. In the house and broken. In the house and missing a life-saving word because Brother So-and-So was preaching. We miss blessings because we have not yet come to our senses. We often allow the distractions of the world to catch us off guard, and we lose our focus. The elder son said a lot without saying a lot. The elder son expressed the issues of his heart without using many words. We apply our false narrative of others and treat them with indifference. The feeling of brokenness speaks to the mind and emotions. Brokenness brings guilt and shame for talking about <u>Sister Joan and Sister Jane</u>. Broken people do not ask for help for fear of being judged, fear that we Christians will not look beyond the image and minister to the need. Brokenness brings embarrassment, too embarrassed to approach <u>Brother Bob and Brother Bill</u> because we just gossiped about <u>them and their wives</u>.

Brokenness exposes shame. Shame on us for lying to each other. Shame on us for gossiping about each other. Shame on us for being impatient and disrespectful to our parents. Shame on us for condoning children's disrespect to adults. Do as I say does not work; you already placed your stamp of approval on your child's disrespectful behavior.

It must be terrifying to be a member of a body of believers and isolated. How hurtful it is to be a member of a family and not valued, simply tolerated, acknowledged only when something is needed of you, tolerated by the people who are supposed to unconditionally love you.

Yes, this hurt is devastating. It silently breaks our hearts, and we continue to be broken and carry its weight.

After all, who would care enough to understand? Which member would be honest enough to admit they are guilty of this behavior? Which member dares to admit the guilt? Which member is seeking to reconcile broken relationships? Who loves God enough to walk with someone through their trauma? Who would listen to them without judgment? Who could love them after knowing their secrets, their hidden sins, and their faults? Who would embrace the authentic them? It is much easier to talk about them, label them, and accuse them, so people remain silent, churched, and broken. Where is my mask?

The elder son, a carnal Christian, if you will, displayed his indifference towards his brother's return. His anger woke up jealousy; his jealousy led to a display of arrogance, which led to his feelings of entitlement. His attitude of unforgiveness told him his brother did not deserve a celebration.

The elder brother needed revenge (as many of us do), revenge for him leaving, revenge for him wasting his money on prostitutes. Revenge for you telling me my truth which I did not like nor wish to hear. I can hear the elder brother's posture of arrogance saying, how dare he get a celebration while I remained working for our father. We lose sight of our blessings when our focus is critical, envious, and indifferent toward others.

We may feel they are not deserving of compassion or kindness. We feel some type of way. But the Father, but God. The elder son was in the house and broken. Churched and broken. Not everyone in the house is going to celebrate you. Maybe the elder brother wanted to go and sow his wild oats but was too afraid to tarnish his pious image as the good son; I don't know. But he was in the house and broken. *Not everyone who is with you is for you, even family.*

The elder son used his indifference as a transitive verb for sin. It is sinful to show a lack of interest in someone in need. It is a sin to dismiss someone with a lack of interest. It is a sin to show a lack of sympathy, disregard, or importance. Indifference is without sincere love or compassion.

When we display this type of behavior, it calls our Christian character into question. It negates our witness.

Why? We were still in our sins when Jesus bled, suffered, and died on our behalf. Jesus was the propitiation, the exchange for our sins. We do not always offer God our very best. One hour of service is too much for some. It does not take all of that, others have said. Other churches get in and out. This may all be true until you need the church to help pay your rent; until you become sick; until you need the prayer warriors of the church; until you need the counsel of the Pastor. Service can last all day when it is for your benefit. Spiritual indifference denies the sovereignty of God. It robs God of his deserved honor and love. Why should we continue to say we love God, <u>whom</u> we have not seen, and not love our neighbors, whom we see daily?

Arrogance masks itself with a lack of humility, prideful, puffed up on the outside, while the inside cries out for help. Arrogance says I am the head of this ministry; you must acknowledge my authority or be dismissed, ignored, and gossiped about. Insecurity is hidden and driven behind the mask of authority. Arrogance calls out on its own, so you may see many cliques within the walls of a church. Arrogance displays one's lack of self-worth. Arrogance blinds us to the fact that it is I, me, and us who need prayer. Arrogance always diverts the other person.

Entitlement is the feeling we are owed something. Each of us experiences the warmth of the sun, however; some believe the purpose of the sun is to shine only on them.

This is the best way I can explain entitlement. Self-serving believers think everything is about them. Self-serving believers manage to reroute a thought, deflect a deed, or deflate an action to be about them. Narcissist through and through. This type of member desires to be the star or the victim of all things inside the walls of the church.

This is the presiding member over when, where, how, and why. It is the mixture that makes it a bad thing. Mix some arrogance with a controlling spirit, and one can guess the toes this member has crushed. We are unable to count the number of members who have left the church and stopped serving God due to our brokenness.

Entitlement then opens the door to low expectations, which mask themselves behind positions and titles we hold in the church; it is through this mask we dismiss others. When we're insecure, how we feel about ourselves shows itself in the treatment of others. (Remember, what is in your heart comes out.) Our actions tell others they are not valued or qualified to work on this committee or perform a task. The issue is not due to their performance, ability, or lack of motivation. The issue is the lack of opportunity extended to them. We will never know the skills sitting dormant in the pews. Unspoken actions speak even louder than words. When a member experiences indifference enough times, the motivation to fellowship dies.

The members of the pews are stifled by the harsh words of certain believers; burdened with their brokenness, they go mute. Mask, anyone? Nita thought when you combine these toxic ingredients with a group of believers inside the walls of a building, you can feel a sense of despair and lack of hope. Is it any wonder why many have given up on the church?

Good news: The real church is not a building. The building is the gathering place. The place where believers assemble to worship. The real church is in your heart; the real church goes wherever you go. You can be churched and broken, but the truth shall set you free.

Promoting gossip about another Christian does not offer the opportunity of healing to the gossiper or the victim. If enough broken members turn on Sister So-and-So with our negative narratives, we then silence, isolate, and ostracize her. We then have created a vicious group of hypocrites within the walls of the building where we assemble to worship.

Gossiping only promotes a protective mechanism for the gossiper. To conceal our issues, we judge and gossip about others, and we remain churched and broken. Our business is to pray for each other and encourage when the opportunity presents itself. Deport yourselves in such a manner that broken members are attracted to you. We oftentimes focus on others to camouflage our brokenness.

We dislike a member because of the things we have heard about them. Those who have a mind of their own should always feel free to use it. Please use your mind as much as possible. Never ignore this fact. The bearer of bad news has just gossiped about you. *If one gossip to you, they will gossip about you*. <u>You are not exempt.</u>
You are either at the table or on the menu. A gossiper needs a listener; if you avail yourself to a gossiper, they then know they can trash talk anyone with you and then go trash talk about you.

<u>We must close off this space.</u>
<u>Lock this door.</u>
<u>Block access to anyone feeling comfortable enough</u> (with us) <u>to talk down about another.</u>
<u>Divert the gossipers' attention to the Word or prayer.</u>

Churched and broken.
We must search our hearts and accept that we are guilty. We must immediately confess and ask God to show us whom he purposed us to be. God's circle of life is humans. We must be sensitive to the Word, study, pray, and apply it. Yes, Christians are human, with a different set of expectations given in the Word. We will never be able

to effectively witness or share the good news in a divided house. We shall continue to hover right at the ceiling. Nita had to accept her responsibility and her role in brokenness. Not an easy pill to swallow, but it must be done'. Nita realized she had to unlearn those habits she had adopted. She also realized she had no desire to hurt people but to use what God had given her to help people. She was driven to uplift others because she knew all too well how it felt to be torn down.

Nita realized God placed her in the business of service, service to God,
service to her family, and service to others. Even when Nita makes a mistake
(and she will), mistakes will keep her in the service of growing.

We serve a God who specializes in the brokenness of his children. He is Master Potter, and we are his clay. He encourages us through his Word. He shapes and molds us for his purpose, his divine purpose.

God is the only specialist who can keep us during a pandemic, keeping us close to him with several virus variants circulating. God is a keeper. Amidst this new norm, the Lord shut the mouth of Nita's asthma. God allows Nita to breathe in the morning, breathe at noon, and breathe at night.

Those with respiratory issues know how that feels. There were many diagnosed with COVID-19 yet still alive to tell it. That is a miracle within itself. God has the final say over all things.

The quarantine forced Nita to deal with herself, her emotions, her motives, and her brokenness. Her biggest challenge was to get out of her way. Nita's flesh was accustomed to being in control, having its way. Nita realized her weapon of warfare was the Word, and through a pandemic, she was fighting for peace, seeking God's peace to renew her mind.

God is a keeper, and Nita wanted him to continue to keep her and her family. Believers, Christians, and God chasers should always offer the best customer service to one another; this carries itself outside of the walls of a building. Charity always begins at home. Unbelievers are watching how we treat each other and interact with each other and want no part of the Body of Christ. Our behavior screams hypocrisy. We must kill this Pharisaic narrative we parade around with. When we come before the Lord to give an account of our stewardship, we shall fall short. It is simple in theory, yet we make it difficult in application to do unto others as God has done unto us. God continues to love on us, despite us.

We shall continue to be broken until we come to our senses and tap into our God, who specializes in brokenness. The only antidote is prayer and the Word, not merely knowing the Word but living the Word. How about knowing the Word and applying it to our everyday lives? How about sharing how the balm in Gilead moved on your behalf?

Compassion, shown by the father of the Prodigal Son, recognized him from a far distance and ran to meet him. He ran so fast that he fell on his neck and kissed him. This is the same love that Jesus showed us at the cross, and this is the same love we must show each other. Believers should ask God to show them how they can be of service. God is waiting with so much love and compassion to heal us of our brokenness and bind us back in alignment with his purpose for our lives.

Protective mechanisms are the masks we use to hide, cover, and camouflage our pain. These mechanisms may be in our speech, actions, attitudes, and posture. No matter the form in which they present themselves, people are attempting to shield themselves from more pain. So many things have infiltrated our hearts and minds, mostly things of no value. Brokenness is the state of this world.

Had it not been for Jesus, we would have self-destructed long ago.

Jesus, our high priest, was touched by the feelings of our infirmities, yet without sin. This means Jesus knows all about us, how we feel and what we think. We have access to God through him. It is through Jesus we are introduced to conquering faith. After all, Jesus conquered the world, and now he sits on the right hand of the Father, making intercession for us. When we put our faith in him, we too are more than conquerors. That type of faith can conquer anything. Through Jesus, we saw healing faith with just a word or a touch. It was through Jesus we saw the determined faith of the woman with the issue of blood.
Job showed us enduring faith. Job went through sickness and death, and trusting God, the author and finisher of our faith, was the way to overcome. Paul taught us we can endure even with a thorn in our side because God's grace is sufficient.

Brokenness is universal. This world and life experiences have left all of us broken in some form. The world's politicians only notice their constituents when their votes or donations are needed. This world is intrinsically driven by greed. How much is enough? For the homeless, life has beaten them down until they are unable to get back up (or choose not to). Those in mental facilities were overwhelmed with the issues of life, and thus their minds tapped out. Others needed an escape from their issues and chose drugs as the means. Whatever the case may be, we all experience brokenness. We have a choice and a way of escaping from our brokenness. Will you accept the way of escape?

Those of us broken and churched found a way of escape offered in the Word and prayer. This way does not make us perfect. It makes us pliable and useable in the hands of Almighty God. You as well can utilize this way of escape; it is free to all.

The Word of God gives us a transfusion of hope. When we get enough of the transfusion, that hope rises and rises and rises. Our perspective is changed, and thus our situations change. Our minds change, our hearts soften, and we began to trust this powerful Word. We trust it so much, it transforms our posture, transforms our attitudes, and transforms our speech. Those of us broken and churched have not fully arrived, but we have come to trust the Word of God. Like a baby learning to walk, it is a process the broken have agreed to take, step by step. We fall, and we get back up. We continue to do this one step, then another step, then another step, continuously holding onto God's Word.

It is key and of most importance that you receive a Word that minister to you. You can hide the Word of God down in your heart and run with that word. Speak that Word over yourself because you know it is not coming back empty. We are trusting the Word of God even in our process. More words, more revelation. Please be careful not to put your mouth on the process of others, as you don't know where God has them or where he is taking them. You know God's Word is going to accomplish what he sent it out to do. No, Christians are not perfect, but we have decided to trust God, no matter what.

It is such a blessing to know our sins are covered by the blood of Jesus. As the songwriter so eloquently phrased:

> We offer Christ to you, oh my brother.
> We offer Christ to you, oh my sister.
> He will give you a brand-new life,
> New life abundantly.
> Oh come, you who are weary and heavy-laden,
> Oh, come, to Christ!

Romans 10:9–10 says, "If thou shalt confess with thy mouth the Lord Jesus, and shalt believe in thine heart that God hath raised him from the dead, thou shalt be saved. For with the heart, man believeth unto righteousness; and with the mouth, confession is made unto salvation."

Here is the issue in a nutshell: There is strength in the posture of brokenness. Why? When we are weak, God is strong. The broken trust in God. Brokenness means we are all out of options. We have no backup plans and no go-to moves. God is our only option.

The broken walk through the valley of the shadow of death, with the assurance that God is with them. The broken have hope. It may only be a slither of hope, but it is hope. The broken are confident that when the enemy comes in like a flood, the Lord will build a standard against him.

God loves the brokenness of his people. Acknowledgment of our brokenness keeps us calling on him, keeps us in a relationship with him, and keeps us connected to him. We are his people and the sheep of his pasture. Contrary to widespread belief, we have not yet arrived. We continue to press toward the mark.

Acknowledgment of our brokenness allows us a posture where God can do his best work in us. Nita thought to herself, *I knew there was something to this brokenness; the spirit of truth prevails as we come forth in our authentic selves.*

The broken can intercede on your behalf to God. Come to your senses and get under the covering of the Word of God. Focus on what your spirit needs, remove your mask, and behold the beauty of the Lord within you.

<u>Psalm 24:7–9</u> says, "Lift up your heads, oh ye gates and be ye lifted ye everlasting doors, and the King of Glory shall come in. Who is this King of Glory? The Lord God strong and mighty, the Lord God mighty in battle. Who is this King of glory? The Lord God, strong and mighty. Lift your heads, oh ye gates, and be ye lifted ye everlasting doors, and the King of glory shall come in!"

The King of Glory, the one who continues to keep a hedge of protection around us. The Lord mighty in battle who shuts the mouth of all diseases. The Lord continues to provide just when you thought there was no way.

<u>Stop looking for perfection in the walls of the church building. Stop looking for perfection in people. All humans are broken. Look to Jesus, who made us whole by his sacrifice on the cross. Jesus presented us to God through his blood.</u>

Jesus is coming back for a church (a group of believers who are dedicated to the spirit) without spot or wrinkle. The physical church is a building where broken believers gather together and call upon the name of Jesus. Come and join us. God's spirit is in our hearts. The spiritual church is where our hearts are fed the word and your Pastor declares the blessings of God over you and your family. Perfection describes one of the character attributes of God.

None of us are perfect. We are peculiar, but not perfect. We have been set apart, but not perfect. We praise and worship God; we are still not perfect.

Instead, look for the fruits of the spirit in people (<u>Galatians 5:22</u>). When you meet someone loving, kind, and patient, inquire of them. There is much to be learned. Find out how and why they came to be so gentle and patient in this present world. Ask them how they came to believe as they do. You will be blessed by their answer.

Stop looking for an image and seek substance. Image is like building your house on quicksand. The image will leave you broken, empty, and standing alone. There is no virtue in the image, no saving grace in the image. The image is worldly. The image is for a show. The image is entertaining to the eyes. There is no concrete substance in the image. Worldly image thrives on the approval of others, which makes it finite, temporary, and fleeting.

Need validation? Go directly to God's Word. The Word will tell you when, where, what, and why. The Word will instruct you on what to do and lay out the promises for your obedience. Got attitude? Come on and lay it at the altar. Whatever your issue may be, the altar of God's heart can make the change. Your attitude will keep you buffering, reliving the same incidents over and over. Allow Jesus to shape and mold that attitude into something he can use.

CHANGE ATTITUDE FOR ALTITUDE

Romans 8:28 says, "And we know that all things work together for good to them that love God, to them who are the called according to his purpose.

All things work together: indifference, controlling spirits, gossiping, and even jealousy. Unpack your issues and bring them to the altar of God's heart. All things. You name it, God can use it and transform it into something good, even attitude. He is doing it for Nita. There are blessings in the presence of God. We can be vulnerable in the presence of God. We can breathe in the fullness of his joy. Cast all your cares, give them to Jesus, and watch him work those things out in your favor.

Brokenness is a good place for God to use us. Within our brokenness lies the humility God needs to see. Our broken place is where the Holy Spirit reveals your assignment. All our isms are addressed in brokenness. God does his best work through our brokenness. We grow leaps and bounds through our brokenness. It is through our brokenness we realize we need the lifesaving help only our God can give.

Thank God for the spirit of brokenness. It is through our brokenness we come into a closer fellowship with our creator. We lose our self-sufficiency, we lose our arrogance, and we lose our will. The purpose of brokenness is to help us realize we can do nothing on our own. Brokenness draws us to the need for God in our life.

Assembling (fellowship) unites us together in our brokenness. Church (the building) offers us a collective place to fellowship, grow with one accord, inspire, and build each other up.

Be our prayers spoken or unspoken, our goal is to be in the will of God.

> Life touches us all.
> No one shall leave this world unscathed.
> Off with the mask.

CHAPTER 8

SUFFERING THROUGH BROKENNESS

What are you wearing?

We often attempt to use our physical strength to approach spiritual battles. The natural is not able to penetrate the spiritual.

Ephesians 6:10–18 breaks down the reason for our armor, how to apply our armor, and when to apply it. Nita paraphrased it.

Paul goes on to say finally, my brothers, be strong in the Lord and the power of his might as described in Colossians 1:11; be strong in God's glorious power with patience, endurance, and joyfulness.

Put on the whole armor of God that we may be able to stand against the tricks, schemes, and subliminal messages of the devil. To stand against the wiles of the devil, we need all of the armor. Why would we need the entire armor? For we wrestle not against flesh and blood (our fight is not with each other; our fight is not with our neighbor, not with another believer or member, and not with any person, for that matter).

Our fight is against the established regiment of the devil: principalities, powers, rulers of the darkness of this world (the world's system), against spiritual wickedness in heavenly places. Paul used the armor of the Roman soldier he was chained to paint the picture. What exactly is Paul saying? He is showing us how to effectively do battle in the spirit realm. We are simply the conduit on earth to what is already going on in the heavenly (high places). Whatever has gone on, is going on, or will go on in the physical is rooted also in the spiritual realm, "wherefore take unto you the whole armor of God that ye may be able to withstand in the evil day; having done all to stand." Paul established where the real battle lay.

Corinthians 10:4 says our weapons of warfare are not carnal but mighty through God to the pulling down strongholds. We must always return to the original start of a thing. (Nita went as far back as she could to determine the origin of her brokenness.) The battle originated in the spirit realm so the only way to fight is with those tools that work in the spirit realm. Ephesians 6:14 tells us to stand with our loins secured with the truth. What is the truth? God's Word.

Christians can move quickly and freely when they know and live the Word of truth. Feet shod (walking and standing on the word) with the preparation of the Gospel of peace; we must be ever ready to share the Good News of Jesus. The Word is our foundational weapon. We are encouraged to stand on God's Word. The Word is a lamp unto my feet and a light unto my path (Psalm 119:105).

"Above all, taking the shield of faith, whereby you will be able to quench all the fiery darts of the wicked." Our faith is complete in the Word. Our shepherd is near, keeping us safe and protected. The helmet of salvation combats our stinking thinking and replaces it with the Word of God. The breastplate guards our hearts against emotional attacks because we have hidden the Word in our hearts so that we might not sin against God. The breastplate secures our hearts on the things that please God. Salvation provides forgiveness for past, present, and future sins. Our greatest weapon is prayer. Prayer should be consistent, intense, and unselfish.

Nita realized that our brokenness is a result of using the wrong armor or not suiting up at all. The penetration of darkness will require us to always be suited in the whole armor. Armor that sheds light into dark places, the dark places of our hearts and minds. When we leave our homes without our armor, we are unable to defend ourselves against the attacks of the devil. We are naked, exposed, unprotected, and broken. Without the armor, we set ourselves up for failure. The enemy loves to keep our minds filled with the worries and cares of this world. The enemy's attacks are subtle and strategic. When the enemy can't get to you, he will attack your family, attack your job, attack your finances, and attack your health.

The ultimate attack is our minds. Let us keep our armor ever-ready.

What are you wearing?

ANOINTED TO GO THROUGH

According to *Job* chapters *1* and *2,* God is:

Omnipresent: He encompasses all space and time.
Omnipotent: He's authoritative and powerful.
Omniscient: He is the total knowledge of all things
Sovereign: He is supreme and excellent.

Job is an excellent example of brokenness.

Job was an honest man inside and out, a man of his word, who was devoted to God and hated evil with a passion (Job was sincere regarding his service to God).

Job was a wealthy man, with seven sons and three daughters; seven thousand heads of sheep; three thousand camels; five hundred teams of oxen; five hundred donkeys; and a huge staff of servants. Job was the most influential man in the entire east. (I believe we would call Job a baller, the renaissance man of his time.) Job's financial status equaled if not surpassed any modern-day billionaire. Job sacrificed for each of his children, just in case one of his children may have sinned or cursed God. Job made a daily habit of this sacrificial atonement for his children. He trusted in the Lord with all his heart.

One day, the sons of God (angels) came to present themselves before God, and the accuser (Satan) came also. God asked Satan where he was coming from, and Satan replied from roaming to and fro throughout the earth (1 Peter 5:8); our adversary, the devil, is a roaring lion walking about seeking whom he may destroy. God asks Satan if he had considered his servant Job (God already knew why the accuser had shown up), and God proceeds to describe Job as blameless, upright, a man who feared God and shunned evil. Satan complains about the hedge of protection God had around Job. Satan went on to tell God how he had blessed the work of Job's hands and everything he possessed. Satan says if God stretched out his hands to strike everything Job possessed, Job would curse God to his face and denounce him.

Satan was telling God we only serve him because of what he does for us and the hedge of protection he keeps around us. Please know the enemy has accused us of only using God and not serving him. The enemy tells God if he removes the hedge of protection from us, we will curse him and die (there is that supposition "if" again).

Remember, God's omniscience gives us the grace to face trials to purify, refine, and enlarge the integrity of our character. God trusts his spirit and the measure of faith he has placed within each of us.

Just as our children seek our permission in the natural realm, the accuser always has to get God's permission before he can touch any of us.

Satan was once an angel and knows how much God loves us. The devil wants to rob us of our spiritual covenant with God, steal our inheritance, and destroy any personal relationship we have with God. The devil was not concerned with Job's wealth or his possessions; the accuser was after Job's integrity towards God.

Satan keeps us distracted by our finances and our health. Our finances and health are the most prevalent of his attacks. We depend on our health and finances to live.

THE FIRST TEST

God says to Satan, "Very well, then, all that he has is in your hands, but on Job himself, do not lay a finger."

Satan's onslaught of attacks came simultaneously, one behind the other:

- oxen and donkeys
- sheep and servants
- camels and servants
- Job's children

Job immediately tore his robe, shaved his head, and fell to the ground in worship.

How do we handle adversity? Most of us question why and feel sorry for ourselves. Our temporary trials of adversity are tailor-made just for us by God himself. God knows you were anointed to go through your designated trial or circumstance. Let us stand with Job in knowing we came into this world naked and naked we will go, and that the Lord giveth and the Lord taketh away. Blessed be the name of the Lord. God trusts us; do we trust him?

"Please know these are traps; the lust of the eyes, the lust of the flesh, and the pride of life" (1 John 1:16–17).

Points to remember:

- God's credentials include the word "Omni," which means "all."
- Job was a righteous and blameless man.

- Satan roams around like a roaring lion.
- Satan's mission is to rob, kill, and destroy.
- God has given us the ability to endure and overcome trials.
- Satan needs God's permission to attack us.

THE SECOND TEST: JOB 2

Satan afflicted Job with leprous sores, complicated with elephantiasis. This disease was thought to be one of the worst of its day. Thus, Job went to isolate himself, like a leper.

He took a piece of broken pottery and went to sit among the ash heaps.

Job's wife, seeing him suffering, sitting in the dust scraping his sores, cries out, "Do you persist in your integrity to God, curse God and die; end your suffering by taking your own life."

The accuser used her as an instrument to grieve her husband rather than comfort him. Job's heart was already at the breaking point now the one closest to him, the one who should have encouraged him and offered him compassion, advised him to take his life. Much like Eve, Job's wife encourages her husband to doubt God in the sovereignty of his divine powers. Ladies, ladies, ladies.

One of the worst hurts in the world is to be disappointed by someone who is supposed to love you, those we have built a relationship with, those we have come to depend upon. When they devastate us, we may be unable to recover. It breaks our spirit. It is important that we women who profess faith in Christ pray for our husbands and sons and encourage them through trial and tragedy.

After all, we did say for better or worse, in sickness and in health until death does us part. It is only when we are practicing the above that we function as true helpmeets.

After enduring all these calamities, Job did not sin by accusing God of doing wrong; he blessed God. In return for Job maintaining his integrity, God blessed him and doubled everything he had before. What are you saying, Nita? Through Job, we learned there is restoration in suffering. There is victory in brokenness.

Commentator, Dr. Linzie McKenzie wrote "the wooing of the Holy Spirit is like a sweet fellowship with a best friend. In this fellowship, we have someone we can totally and completely rely on. The wooing of God is like a soft gentle tug on the strings of our hearts."

Pastor Jeff said in between the prophecy and the promise is our process. Our process is a series of events with an intended end. Your process includes all the trials and experiences God has purposely walked you through, to overcome. We are not able to reach the promise before we complete the process.

God woos us with his spirit so we may woo others to him, with the fruits of the spirit. Jesus showed his agape love towards us on the cross: unconditional, no strings attached. His love and his joy are unspeakable. Peace as told in Psalm 23; he leads us beside the still waters. He bids all who are weary and weighed down with the cares of this world to come, and he will give you rest. He not only offers rest but promises to keep us in perfect peace, a peace we are not able to understand. Tugging at our heartstrings with brand-new mercies every day. He is so patient, gentle, and kind toward us. Who could ask for a better father, dad, Savior, or healer?

God woos us in through prayer. Our trysting place demands our heart, mind, and spirit. Our secret place shuts out the distractions and noise of the world and shuts us in. Our secret closet provides an atmosphere of intimate communication with God. Hebrews 11:6 says we must believe he is a rewarder and believe he will reward those who diligently seek him. Through prayer, we seek to grow our relationship with God. Through prayer, we receive his supernatural help.

Nita came to understand the protocol power of prayer through her brokenness.

Repentance: I come asking for forgiveness for all things that do not bring glory to your name. 1 John 1:9 says if I confess my sins, you are faithful and just to forgive me of my sins and to cleanse me from all unrighteousness.

Adoration: Psalm 46:10 tells us to be still and know that he is God; he will be exalted among the heathen, he will be exalted in the earth. We respectfully acknowledge God as the supreme dominion over us. We bless you, precious Lord, with our whole hearts.

Thanksgiving: I'm grateful for all God has done, is doing, and will do in my life.

Then I'm able to petition God. Prayer transfers my worries and concerns to God. Prayer builds my faith in God and strengthens my relationship with him. Prayer offers me the opportunity to share my thoughts, feelings, fears, and desires with God, void of judgment. Prayer enhances my happiness, increases my peace, and reduces my stress.

Praise and worship are my appreciation of God for who he is and what he has done. Praise is the highest form of respect. When God inhabits the praise of his people, worship follows unto the almighty God, our high priest, abba father, Jehovah Rapha, our Shepherd. We audibly acknowledge his deity in our relationship. We can express our love and adoration to God.

Worship allows us to address his worthiness and the virtue of who he is. Worship is our respect and love for God, all blended.

Philippians 1:6 says being confident of this, that he who began a good work in us will carry it on to completion until the day of Christ Jesus. This "good work" we are confident in is our assigned process. Our life experiences are preplanned according to the ability God placed within us. We win either way.

Nita realized that God had been wooing her for a long time. God used grief, anger, and attitude to get her attention. His Word is true; all things do work together for the good. Nita's praise and worship simultaneously pour out tears of laughter. His mercy has been hilariously overwhelming, as it brings Nita to tears of joy and happiness.

Nita was initially apprehensive of her praise because it was different. Her only concern is to be in the will of God, to be used for his service.

Brokenness will cause you to give naysayers more of your attention than they deserve. Today is so very different due to God's wooing. The Holy Spirit encourages Nita to let go; "I got you," he says. The Holy Spirit reminded Nita her trials and experiences were tailored for her growth and that her response should be different. Nita vividly remembers that God was with her during every valley-of-death experience.

God's wooing gave Nita the strength to be a caregiver during sickness and the strength to endure disappointments. Not one naysayer during her trials, just her and God. She witnessed more sickness and death than she cared to mention.

Camouflage it as she tried, the residue of trauma was still in her spirit. During one season, death continued to show up. God continued to woo Nita through the times of death to be the strength to others facing their mortality.

"Absent from the body is to be present with the Lord" is ever so true, but the pain is also real and present. When Nita yielded to the process of death, God made the pain easier to bear. Nita realized it was God who kept her from losing her mind. It was God who protected her from dangers, seen and unseen. It was God who kept making a way when there was no way. It was God who continued to show her favor when others dismissed her, tolerated her, and gut-punched her. God was there all the time, wooing Nita back to him.

Nita fell in love with God's wooing compassion and consideration for her. The Word of God continues to lure Nita closer and closer to him. God uses various means to woo us back to him. He wants us to understand his love and challenges us to adopt the very same characteristics. Go into all the world and share God's goodness with others.

Our faith makes things possible, not easy.

> There once was a man who had nothing for his family to eat. He had an old shotgun and three bullets. So he decided that he would go out and kill something for dinner. As he went down the road, he saw a rabbit; he shot at the rabbit and missed it. Then he saw a squirrel; he fired a shot at the squirrel and missed it too.
>
> As he went further, he saw a wild turkey in a tree, and he had only one bullet, but a voice came to him and said, "Pray first, aim high, and stay focused."

However, at the same time, he saw a deer, which was a better kill. He brought the gun down and aimed at the deer.

But then he saw a rattlesnake between his legs, about to bite him. So he naturally brought the gun down farther to shoot the rattlesnake.

The voice spoke again and stated, <u>"I said, 'Pray first, aim high, and stay focused."</u> So the man decided to listen to the voice.

He prayed, then aimed the gun high up in the tree and shot the wild turkey. The bullet bounced off the turkey and killed the deer.

The handle fell off the gun and hit the snake in the head and killed it.

And when the gun went off, it knocked him into a pond.

When he stood to look around, he had fish in all his pockets, a deer, and a turkey to eat.

<u>The snake (Satan) was dead simply because the man listened to God.</u>

MORAL OF THE STORY

Pray first before you do anything and aim high for your goals. Stay focused on God. Never let others discourage you about your past. The past is exactly that; the past.

Live every day, one day at a time, and remember that only God knows your future and he will not put you through any more than you can bear.

Do not look to others for your blessings but look to the hills for help; be ready to walk through those doors he will open and stand under those windows to catch the overflow of blessings.

Wait, be still and patient: keep God first, and everything else will follow.

EPILOGUE

In retrospect, Nita thought the days of wearing patent leather shoes and itchy dresses were not so bad. Nita's brother, Lewis saw something in Nita she needed to change. She needed an attitude adjustment and a renewed mind. Nita's heart needed to be purged with hyssop. The muscles of her spirit needed maintenance.

Yes, Nita loved hard from a good place, but her love often came with unspoken strings. Yes, Nita was loyal, dependable, and trustworthy, but her posture of indifference came across as critical and punitive. Guilty was Nita in returning a more intense version of whatever was given to her. Guilty of not taking a road at all, high or low, but meeting a situation head-on. She was guilty of rebuking others as if swatting flies. There was no hesitation in putting you in your place if you stepped to Nita wrong. Her attitude was her mask of brokenness, blocking gifts and promises God had in store for her. Nita is in her process, and the Holy Spirit is navigating her through the process of brokenness. Meditation on the Word helped Nita to realize her assignment as an ambassador for Christ, demanded a change of character. Our Christ-like behavior should be the first thing people see.

How can we win souls when we are not invested? Someone, somewhere, needs our testimony to be free. Someone, somewhere, needs to see our behavior live up to our verbal hype. Someone, somewhere, needs to see more than an image in our witness. Change.

Nita accepted her assignment to encourage and uplift in the same manner she was enlightened. God offered several platforms of evangelism, and she only needed to open her eyes. The Holy Spirit assured her she could drop the mask of attitude.

No need to camouflage who you are while in the Word. You can be as vulnerable as you need to be, whenever you need to be. The Holy Spirit was there to navigate her to the next season of her life. Our storms in life are under the master's control. He controls the winds and the waves. Peace moves at his command. He says you are free to be whom I created you to be before he formed you in your mother's womb. Nita wished to beg her brother for forgiveness, forgiveness for purposely disobeying him.

Forgiveness for the times she challenged his authority. Forgiveness for manipulating his words in her favor. Forgiveness for calling her brother a bully. Forgiveness for the punitive posture she displayed to others. Forgiveness for the stealthy motives hiding in her heart. Nita thought her brother would be so happy and proud of her new mindset and her new attitude. He would be happy to see how far she had come in her journey. Her spirit was sorry she was unable to share this revelation with her brother, who had since passed away.

Nita decided to keep herself at the altar of God's heart and remain in his Word. It is through the Word Nita could continue to remove the mask, along with those patent leather shoes. The need for less regimented thinking was found in the Word. Through the Word of God, she could forgive the indifference she experienced from a teacher or a boss. The Word is teaching her that prayer, supplication, and thanksgiving can eliminate her anxiety. Through the Word, she learned to examine herself in challenging authority. Good leaders must also be good followers.

Nita learned when adults remove themselves from a place of respect, we must still respect them, even when we do not agree with them. Her regimented way of thinking, inherited from her father, came across as harsh and punitive to others. She is learning to tone that down to be more effective. It is okay to be different.

Nita decided to stay with a repentant heart because the healing process of brokenness is lifelong. She could bask in that same compassion as shown to the Prodigal Son. She thanked God for his permissive and divine will in her life.

Everyone has something to offer, nuggets and drops of wisdom. Nita is learning to glean or pull from all God sends her way, always the student.

Nita so eloquently recited her Easter speech address. _John 3:16_ says, "For God so loved the world that he gave his only begotten son in that who so ever would believe in him should not perish but have everlasting lasting life." Amen.

Nita and Ann went on to enjoy their Easter basket, eating as much candy as they could.

God chose to use Nita's brokenness for her growth, to build his kingdom, to encourage those assigned to her, and to share with others what he has given to her. God's Word is showing Nita how to look past the negative and see the good in a person or situation. She is growing in leaps and bounds. Embrace your brokenness; he will do the same for you. Thank God for his love, even in our brokenness.

Off with the mask.

If my life was a credit report and I was trying to obtain salvation, based on my score, I wouldn't get it. My history shows that I've been delinquent in praise and past due in prayer, my worship has been in collections, and I've missed a few payments or only paid <u>half</u> a tithe (you know how we put twenty dollars in the basket and feel like we've done God a favor).

Not to mention that my debt-to-income (sin-to-blessings) ratio is <u>high</u>.

But I thank God I was able to file bankruptcy through his forgiveness, and <u>it</u> <u>cleared</u> <u>me</u> of all my debt (sin).

Now I have a cosigner (Jesus) whose score is flawless, with not one blemish (sin) on his report.

So now, I qualify for everything.

<u>Most</u> <u>importantly,</u> I've inherited eternal life, and I didn't have to put one penny down.

All my closing costs were covered when Jesus laid down His life for me.

I hear that my future home has all the upgrades too.

Hardwood floors? Please. I'll be walking on gold.

Churched and broken is where you can find me.

Thank you, Lord, for grace and mercy in my brokenness.

Be all glory, honor, dominion, and power, forever and ever. Amen.

My prayer for *the Churched and Broken* is that it blesses you to make the necessary changes needed in your life.

ACKNOWLEDGMENTS

Pastor Gregory D. Hunter, you are truly dedicated and excited about the Word of God.

Your sermons are filled with your godly excitement. It is such a joy listening to you and the exhortations of the ministers. Olivet Oakland is a church that promotes the Word of God. The preached Word drew me to Olivet. The music ministry provided the gravy.

Each Sunday, your sermon confirmed thoughts I had written the week before. How could this be? You did not know, nor had I shared my topic. We knew your sermons were for our growth, although sometimes it felt as if you were operating on us without anesthesia (smile). Cuts of healing. The Holy Spirit was giving me confirmation through your sermons. I have truly been blessed.

You continued to feed and support your members, even while going through your loss. Our neediness often made us forget your pain as you silently endured the grief process. You did not stop being a pastor, even after your loss. You did not have the option to stop. We thank you for your godly posture during your loss. We respect your dedication to your craft. This speaks volumes of your character and the anointing in your life. I thank God for your growth.

God blessed your spiritual act of genius to push your congregation to new heights of growth in the Word. You have shown yourself as the ultimate leader in pioneering your members through this pandemic and keeping us fed with the Word.

5:00 a.m. Payer Line
Mornings in the Word
Sunday's Live Stream
Senior Prayer Wednesday
GYM (Bible Study)
Word Handlers Workshop

Thank you for listening to the Word of God, thank you for following the Holy Spirit, and thank God for giving you a heart for his Word. As the oil continues to flow from the top, I thank God for the drops that fall, even on me.

I pray God continues to bless and keep you.

Special Thanks to the Ministers

Pastor (Point of No Return) Jeffrey Williams, the Recondition Church, Tracy, CA.

Minister of High Praise Adedra Lee, Olivet, Oakland, California

Minister (Authentically) Tamara Edwards, Olivet, Oakland

Minister (Lil' Peter) Portia McGhee, Olivet, Oakland

Elder (Governor) Darryl Norman, Olivet, Oakland

Elder (Do This in Remembrance of Me) Mazie Greer, Olivet, Oakland

Now, unto him who can keep you from falling, and to present you faultless before the presence of his glory with exceeding joy; to the only wise God our Savior, be glory, majesty, dominion, and power, both now and forever. Amen.

May God continue to bless and keep each of you.

This book challenges only to evoke change, off with the mask.

A WORD FROM THE AUTHOR

Hallelujah. I'm happy to share my second book, which targets the spiritual brokenness of believers. Uncover our pre-pandemic masks. Believers have worn masks for years to hide their pain. My book, *Churched, and Broken* offers the needed safe place to identify, acknowledge, and make the needed changes to your spiritual freedom. Come along with the book's character, Nita, as she returns to her childhood to discover and reveal the origin of her brokenness.

I am so excited for the breakthrough of the readers. God bless.

Printed in the United States
by Baker & Taylor Publisher Services